FROM GUARDS TO GUARDIANS

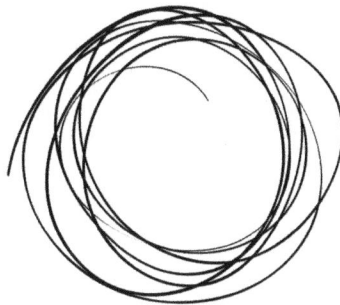

REBUILDING PRISONS
FROM THE GROUND UP

Nicole Daedone

soulmaker | PRESS

soulmakerpress.com

soulmaker | PRESS

ISBN: 978-1-961064-14-0

CONTENTS

Starting Your Journey

Lessons

The Journey Continues

TESTIMONIAL QUOTES
ABOUT THE PROGRAM

"For me, this program would have been a good resource for me to lean on to help others because in my profession, I have lost good friends. I have seen families be destroyed. This program could have given me a great resource so I can tell somebody, 'Hey, did you read this? Do you know of this program? This can help.' So this program to me could have maybe saved some lives, before they decided to take their own."

-Anthony Gangi, New Jersey State Corrections,
20+ years as a CO

"I believe the program falls under that category Chicken Soup for the Soul. *The program is exactly that, it's a medication. It's something we can read and put into our mind and body and spirit and use to turn our lives around, turn our work environment into a positive place. If we had more programs that bridge the gap and educate Officers on how to come forward and express their thoughts, express their opinions, and to express what is going on in their lives. It helps them to get it out of their system. That you can get through these trials and tribulations and never allow yourself to think that you're alone."*

-Gary York, Florida State Corrections Department,
Corrections1 Columnist, 28 years as a CO

"First and foremost, From Guards to Guardians *serves to remind us that no matter our role, we are all human. As such, we need to recognize our limitations and strive to overcome them on a personal level."*

-Keith Hellwig, Wisconsin State Corrections, 36+ years as a CO

"I think if the Guards to Guardians *program was available when I was working the tiers, it would have been absolutely life changing for me. I've been through some traumatic events in my life and I think this would have given me tools I need to cope with those things."*

-Greg Piper, Kansas State Corrections, 16 years as a CO

"When I started going through these questions, I thought this should be integrated in mandatory training. It's honest self-evaluation. I'm actually jealous of the Officers getting it now, because I would have loved to have had it when I started my career."

- Steve Maynard, North Carolina Corrections Department, 15 years as a CO

WELCOME TO *FROM GUARDS TO GUARDIANS*

The Unconditional Freedom Project was developed with a vision of turning prisons into monasteries, where the experience of incarceration becomes an opportunity for people to undertake the journey of connecting to their soul and discovering unequivocal freedom—a journey we call *soulmaking*.

Yet, within monasteries, monks are not left to their own devices to do their work as they will. Instead, they function under the guidance of priests and guides who act as mentors in their unfolding. For those who are incarcerated, these are Corrections Officers. In wishing for prison residents to have the opportunity to grow from prisoners to penitents, we must also support COs in their own soulmaking—in their transformation from a guard into the Guardian.

COs venture into spaces most of us dare not tread, to do a job most of us could not do. They see things most of us could not imagine, and endure experiences that would break the rest of us into pieces. In fact, COs suffer some of the highest rates of PTSD of any career, including police officers.

Corrections Officers put walls between themselves and the danger they face daily. While this is helpful on the job, spending as much time as they do in these conditions, many COs report that they wind up having trouble accessing their emotions, positive or negative, and that their lives are lacking in intimacy.

From Guards to Guardians: Rebuilding Prisons from the Ground Up (Abridged Version) is a book for Corrections Officers, designed to restore your sense of humanity and spark the flame for a new vision for the profession, going beyond security and confinement in to the cultivation of flourishing individuals. This book provides the tools to access the humanity required to thrive in your life, both on the job and at home, and imbue your profession with a purpose that creates better outcomes for everyone and allows for a healthy, sustainable life for you. Officers go from security and peacekeeping, to Guardians, keepers of this space of penitence, who stand watch and support the transformation of people in their darkest days. Guardians shape the future of our country.

This program was created to honor Correctional Officers, the people who put their lives on the line in order to provide safety. We want to do this by being honest, and by admitting that as a culture, we have abandoned the Correctional Officer as well as the prison resident. While you must be strong and stoic on the job, it is our work to help lift your burden. Who ensures the safety of the Correctional Officer, while they are ensuring that everyone—both inside and outside of prison—feels safe? Who will pay attention to the burden and the stress that you carry in the name of duty—a duty that goes well beyond what humans are meant to hold alone? This program is our "thank you" to the Correctional Officer. And our apology for what we left them to hold.

With the readings and integration exercises in this book, Officers can start to dismantle the armor that has hardened their physical, mental, emotional, and spiritual body over time, allowing for healing, creativity, and contribution within themselves and those around them.

HOW TO GET THE MOST
OUT OF THIS BOOK

From Guards to Guardians: Rebuilding Prisons from the Ground Up (Abridged Version) is broken down into an introduction followed by four lessons. Each lesson concludes with integration questions.

The lessons build on one another, so while you can flip around leisurely, it's suggested that on your first read you move from one lesson to the next, in sequential order. Once you have completed the book, you may find yourself revisiting certain sections or reading the entire book again, from start to finish. There may be some parts that you come back to on a regular basis.

This book takes you on a journey of soulmaking, diving inside of yourself. We understand that some of this material is difficult. It is okay to take your time.

You can study this book alone, in a group, with a friend, or reach out to the Guards to Guardians program director to work with a CO mentor.

At the end of each lesson is a series of questions—the integration exercises—that will help you connect more deeply with what you have just read and with the pieces you hold inside that are ready to be seen. Your soul has been waiting to talk to you. These questions are designed to help the conversation.

You can start by asking yourself one question each day. Take your time with this process. Answers may appear immediately, and they may not. One answer may appear, but may continue to unfold over days, weeks, months, or a lifetime. Also, answers from the soul do not look like answers from the brain. You may suddenly think of song lyrics, a book you read in the past, something a friend once told you, or an image you saw spray-painted on a wall 16 years ago. You may go outside and see something in nature that catches your attention.

Remember that the soul, while it's delighted to communicate with you, does not do straightforward Q&A. It will likely take some practice to learn to listen to the language of your soul. Don't worry. With time and practice, you will become expert at it, because your soul has inexhaustible patience and resources, and it wants nothing more than to connect with you.

Soulmaking is very much like a video game where once you "solve" one level and have one of those satisfying "ah-ha!" moments, another level or series of questions or puzzles presents itself. At times, this can feel frustrating or discouraging, but remember the goal is not completion, it is mastery, and that is a lifelong process.

Relax, breathe, and let it all unfold.

To learn more about the program or find ways to go deeper, visit **www.unconditionalfreedom.org/guardians** or email **info@unconditionalfreedom.org**.

"Captain once told me, 'Society may often forget about the gatekeeper known only as a corrections [or] detention officer, but what would society do without him or her at the gate?'"

~Jerome, former CO and former Marine

INTRODUCTION: A TRANSFORMATIVE JOURNEY

Embark on your journey of soulmaking as you embrace your role as Guardian. Connect with your inner self, tap into the power of love, and begin to create a change inside yourself and the prison environment.

What would society do without you, the keeper of the gate? We owe you a debt of gratitude that is rarely, if ever, acknowledged. Your job is one that most of us could not do. You regularly encounter situations that many of us have never seen.

Yet as potent and impactful as you already are, there's potential for something more. For a life that's *more* fulfilling and satisfying than the one you currently experience—a way to make your work more meaningful and for you to make more of a difference, for yourself and the rest of the world.

Maybe you've sensed this somewhere inside you. Maybe you've looked around and wondered what it's all for—this confinement, the frustration of watching people locked away from society while the world passes them by, and you along with them. Maybe you've long known there must be a better way. A way beyond just punishment. A way that heals instead of hurts. A way that connects instead of rejects. A way that creates real solutions.

An online job description for a Correctional Officer states that a CO is "responsible for enforcing the rules and maintaining routines." Yes, that is the job of a *guard*. But a *Guardian* does much more. When a guard becomes a Guardian, a prison resident is empowered to become a *penitent*.

The word "penitent" refers to someone who demonstrates sorrowful remorse, someone who atones for past deeds and actions and experiences a true change of heart. The word "penitentiary" was originally intended as a place where people would go to experience a transformation based on self-realization. That's the kind of penitentiary we envision—a place where prison residents are supported to be penitents, and you, as their keeper, their mentor, serve as a Guardian who enables this process.

We describe the journey of the penitent, and of anyone who undergoes this kind of deep personal transformation, as the journey of *soulmaking*. Instead of simply passing time and enduring punishment, an incarcerated individual has the opportunity to connect with their soul, and to allow an atmosphere and attitude of freedom and flourishing inside them. You, in your role as Guardian, can help to support their transformation and, in the process, engage in your own soulmaking journey.

In this relationship, inmates and guards become the fullest versions of what they can be. It's a mutually dependent, mutually beneficial relationship in which each party recognizes and honors the other. That may sound like some kind of impossible fantasy. But everything that's ever come to be a reality originated in someone's imagination. From inventions such as the automobile and the lightbulb, to shifts in human relationships, everything we imagine can—in the right conditions and if we know how to nurture and shape it—come to be.

Let's be clear: There's nothing wrong with you or the work you've been doing. But things could be different. You don't have to endure such trauma without any support. Your work doesn't have to go unappreciated and unrecognized. You don't have to suffer.

As former CO Brian says, "I became jaded by the system when I realized we're not about correcting; we're about making sure they don't get out until they're supposed to. That diminishes our role as Correctional Officers." The way the prison system has been operating ignores your true capacity and capability. It sells short your gifts and your abilities.

Throughout the prison system, there are COs who are already acting as Guardians. Here's one example described by a woman who was visiting her father in prison:

My dad was in the prison hospital, dying of liver cancer. When you have this form of cancer, you swell up and fill with fluids. There had been shackles on his wrists and ankles, and I could see where the swelling had caused them to cut through his skin. He looked like he was still wearing the shackles even though they'd taken them off because by that point, he was in a coma.

I was standing there by his bed and I heard this voice apologizing to him. Then I realized it was my voice. I was apologizing. I don't know why, I just knew that it was important for him, before he died, to hear an apology. As for what for, I could figure that out later. Even if I never did, it didn't matter.

An apology sounds especially confusing if you know that this man, my father, was in prison for child molestation. People who are imprisoned for this, it's pretty well known how they're treated—like animals. Really, it would be considered inhumane to treat animals in this way. Often, they are just beaten to a pulp, or kept in isolation. It's like this one thing that most of the guards and inmates agree on— pedophiles are not human.

I was standing there next to my father's hospital bed and I was just shaking. There was a guard standing there in the room with me and he was what you'd expect most guards to be. Very stoic. Very masculine. Very stiff and formal. And there I was, coming apart at the seams. I felt safer in some way having him there, but I also felt embarrassed. But then something happened. I looked at the guard and all of a sudden, it was like he let me see him—the real him. He let me see that he felt pain, too.

Finally, he spoke. "Your father was a good man."

I stared. "Tell me more," I said.

The guard paused for a moment. "He was funny," he said. "He would make me laugh." He was silent again for a few moments, then added, "As much as a guard and an inmate can be friends, we were friends."

I knew what he said was not right. Not that it wasn't true, but that he wasn't supposed to be talking to me in this way. He was breaking protocol. He was willing to do the "wrong" thing in order to do the honorable thing. This man was more than a guard, he was a Guardian. Because with those words, he set me free.

Before that day, I hated that man. I hated guards. They were people who were hurting my father, who saw him as less than human. But that day, that man showed me his heart—a heart that chose this role. He stepped out of the space of terrified activation where a guard is afraid he, one of his colleagues, or an inmate will be injured or killed and instead, there in that room, showed me the truth of himself.

In order for being a Guardian instead of a guard to become the norm rather than the exception, you are required to choose, to commit, and to act, just as this CO did.

The role of Guardian is for you to embrace and embody. It's not an easy undertaking, but we're here to help.

Soulmaking is the language we speak and a journey we know.

We know that building a soul is the work of a lifetime. It is without end. None of us ever will be finished. Our task will never be complete, but this is the work we're all here to do, and it's the work that must be done if we want to live a full and rich life in which we learn, grow, and thrive, and where we achieve our potential. Every single one of us has tremendous potential, because we were born with it. It's all already inside us. Soulmaking is about connecting with that potential, and actualizing it.

While each person's soulmaking journey is unique, there are principles and practices—the necessary components of soulmaking—that apply to us all. That's what we'll be sharing with you in these pages.

Unconditional Freedom

That woman who visited her dying father in prison was one of us. That story, her experience, is part of the genesis of our work to serve you, the CO.

The aim of the Unconditional Freedom Project is to restore dignity to members of society who have been canceled—those who have been marginalized or in some other way cast out, including individuals who are incarcerated. Our goal is to provide prison residents with nourishment and support to help restore their sense of dignity and worthiness so that they are able to find meaning and purpose in their lives. It's also to provide support for their mentors—the COs who care for and protect them every day.

When we launched this program, we wondered what our world would be like if prisons functioned more like monasteries. To some, that might sound ludicrous. But is it a coincidence that in many monastic traditions, monks' quarters are called cells? Maybe not. To you as a CO, comparing a prison to a monastery probably makes more sense than it does to others, because you've likely seen firsthand at least one incredible transformation that occurred when an inmate chose to view their incarceration as an opportunity for deep self-exploration.

In 2020, with our book *The Art of Soulmaking for the Incarcerated*, we introduced women residents at a state prison facility in California to the types of practices monks use—including meditation and yoga—to experience personal transformation. Additionally, participants were paired with volunteers—people from local community centers, senior homes, donors, and others across the country—with whom they could correspond throughout their journey. When we first launched the program, we immediately had a waitlist of people in prison who were interested in the program. We expanded our volunteer program to be able to provide each prison resident who wanted to participate with a pen pal.

The next phase of our work involved turning our attention to our most critical partners in this work—you, the COs.

After all, who are in closer, more regular contact with prison residents than COs? Who play a greater role in influencing their experience of incarceration? Our mission is to help turn prisons into monasteries, but monks need mentors. They need guides. They need Guardians. And you deserve to fill that noble and lofty role. To realize the full power and beauty of your own soul as you care for others.

Remembering Your True Self

Hanuman is a god in the Hindu religion who is known for his extreme strength and courage as well as his selfless service. But Hanuman wasn't always this version of himself—like Wolverine, Batman, Iron Man, Captain Marvel, or any other of today's comic book heroes (and heroes in real life), Hanuman has an origin story.

He had a mortal mother, but his father was Vaya—the wind god, who gave Hanuman the ability to fly. One day, young Hanuman awoke hungry from a deep sleep and found that his mother, who usually provided him with sweet, delicious fruit to eat, was gone. He looked around but couldn't find any fruit to eat. When he looked up to the sky, he saw the most beautiful, delectable piece of fruit he'd ever seen. But in reality, the "fruit" he saw was the sun. Hanuman took off into the sky to grab the fruit, but Indra, the god of Heaven, seeing him charge toward the sun, cast a lightning bolt at Hanuman that struck him in the jaw. When Vaya, Hanuman's father, saw this, he became so angry that he struck back at all the gods, entering their bodies and making them ill. Meanwhile, Hanuman slunk off to a cave to recover from the lightning strike. Feeling bad for what had happened to him (and wanting to appease his father), the gods gathered around Hanuman and gave him a powerful assortment of gifts, including extraordinary strength, knowledge, wisdom, the ability to make himself as large or small as he wanted, and immortality.

But in his youth, Hanuman was mischievous, and started to abuse his powers by using them to play pranks. The gods became tired of Hanuman's relentless antics and prayed to Brahman, the supreme god, for help. Brahman and the gods then put a curse on Hanuman that made him forget his superpowers. And so, for many years, Hanuman had no awareness of his true abilities—until one day when others who knew about his gifts decided to remind him of his powers.

Maybe like Hanuman you, too, have forgotten who you are. Maybe spending so much time working in prison, in an atmosphere of confinement and stress, you've forgotten your pure heart and your gifts. Maybe that knowledge has become buried underneath the burdens you bear day after day.

Whether you know it or not, your true abilities and your true calling—something the ancient Greeks called your *genius*—lies deep inside you; it's something you can never lose. But years of hard work, doing a critical job without acknowledgment, without many tools or resources, may have left you feeling anxious and dejected.

Maybe you feel discouraged and ineffective, or as if all you're doing day after day is just trying to hold back a dam that could break at any second. You're not alone. Many COs say they rarely feel safe at work. For hours at a time everything is calm, then suddenly there's a fight, alarms are going off, or you encounter someone who has taken their own life. At the end of the day, you're expected to flip a switch in your mind and go home, talk to your spouse or play with your kids as if everything is fine.

The cycle of going from static routine to sudden fear, shock, or grief with little or no support or recovery time can dysregulate your nervous system. Over time, the way the world looks can start to shift. You may begin to lose your positive outlook and the belief that you can be an instrument of change. Maybe you start to doubt that what you do makes a difference. Your dream and your desire to serve becomes clouded as you struggle to remember why you're doing all this. Is it the money? The security? Trying to create a life for your family?

Under such stress and strain, it's easy to forget. And as you've undoubtedly seen for yourself, far too many of your colleagues don't make it. They drink or do anything else they can to numb the pain and the rage, and some of them, feeling totally hopeless, take their own lives. Statistics show that, on average, every week three COs die by suicide.

But there's a way back.

There's a greater opportunity and experience awaiting you.

There's a way to remember.

To find it, let's begin at the beginning.

The Heart of a CO

How do people become COs? Many, like former CO Jerome, who is quoted at the start of this Introduction, first served in the military. Whether they served in the armed forces or as police officers, or traveled some other path to arrive at their position in the prison system, one thing most COs have in common is that they came to this work out of a desire to serve. Not only do they want to protect their community—to *guard the gate*, as Jerome's captain put it—most also want to protect the prison residents themselves.

Because what goes on behind prison walls is something most of us don't see; we derive our opinions largely from media portrayals of COs. Unfortunately, and as you no doubt know, COs are often shown as passive and disconnected at best, and abusive, sadistic, or corrupt at worst. As Brian, a former CO with sixteen years' experience, said, "There is so much negative stigma of what goes on behind these walls. Most things people are told that go on in Corrections are overblown, and people judge us on that false narrative."

What we rarely, if ever, see are your victories. We don't see you having meaningful conversations with the people you protect, talking them down when they're having a bad day and feeling like they're going to lose it. We don't see stories of COs like Kyle, who said that when he worked as a CO in Arizona, he focused on being a problem-solver for inmates. "If I saw an inmate had a problem or was frustrated about something, my first reaction would be to talk—to get him to explain what had happened so that, together, we could find a solution." We don't see you putting yourself in harm's way to prevent a fight. And we don't see the struggles you have or the despair you experience when you find yourself at home trying to relate to your spouse and yelling at your children as if they were inmates. We don't understand how hard it is to be gentle and compassionate and greet your family with a loving heart when you've spent the entire day dealing with the constant threat of violence.

As former CO Brian describes it, "We all know when we sign on that this job comes with physical danger, but they don't tell you about the danger to your mind and spirit. Over time, you begin to lose your natural tendencies toward human empathy and compassion. A part of your humanity is slowly whittled away."

To engage in this work and do it well, especially over the long term, requires not just a calling, but superhuman abilities—some might even say the abilities of a superhero. Under the extreme duress you experience from day to day (or night to night), you have to focus entirely on survival skills. You've become caught in a cycle of diminishing returns as the fulfillment you once anticipated or experienced from your work has declined, or maybe disappeared entirely. According to a national survey of COs, ninety-one percent agreed with the statement, "PTSD is a serious and pervasive issue within Corrections."

When we become fixated on survival, we develop a kind of tunnel vision. It becomes harder to see a way out, and to imagine how things might be different. The vision you had when you started this work is now a distant memory. But your gifts, who you are, and that inherent desire to serve, are all still inside you.

What's a CO like Kyle actually doing when he engages meaningfully with inmates on a personal level—relates to them as one human being to another? What superhuman power is he invoking? It's not vague or mysterious, but it's much bigger than all of us. That power is love. If the idea of loving a prison resident sounds strange, think for a moment about the incredible transformative power that love has had in your own life—when you've received a word of kindness from a friend, or even a stranger, an embrace from a parent, an "I do" from a spouse, or looked into the eyes of your child. Love changes us. Part of your special power and unique gift is the opportunity to offer love to people society has deemed unlovable.

Of course, no one's actually unlovable; it's a choice to see people that way. But it takes an exceptionally powerful person to be willing to offer compassion and care to those who've been judged unworthy, who may have done things so horrifying and appalling that it's tough to even think about them. That power is part of the special genius inside you.

From Guards to Guardians

Once Hanuman was reminded of his abilities, he learned how to engage his skills along with his compassion, and he became a kind of servant-hero. That's a transformation you, too, can make.

Everything you need to begin is in these pages. We'll share myths and stories both new and old, science, and perhaps most important, insights from other COs who've shared many of your experiences. We'll also offer exercises, reflections, insights, and practices that will help you connect, or reconnect, with your true self. You'll develop the ability to access resources that will help you process the stress and strain of the work you do. And you'll learn how to open to, and connect with, the intelligence of your heart.

In the 1950s, a crew of workers were tasked with moving a statue of the Buddha to a temple in Bangkok, Thailand. It was a beautiful statue, covered with stucco and colored glass, but also exceptionally heavy and difficult to maneuver. As the workers struggled and strained to move the statue, a piece of the stucco was accidentally chipped away, revealing a shocking surprise. Underneath the stucco and glass, the Buddha was made entirely of gold. As it turned out, about two hundred years before, the monks had covered the statue with ordinary materials to conceal its true worth. Today, the "Golden Buddha" sits in the temple in Bangkok, brilliant and shining, its true nature having been lovingly uncovered.

Often, our true nature remains covered until the time is right to reveal it, until, as we are struggling, some part of our outer shell breaks free. Those you take care of *are* the Golden Buddha, and so are you.

Through this process of "uncovering," your work will shift. You'll find that you relate differently to both the prison residents and your peers in ways that feel more effective, impactful, and empowering, to you and to others. Again, we're not here to *fix* you, because there's nothing wrong with you. And we're not here to tell you who and how to be. Instead, this book is meant to help you uncover something already inside you, and you'll do that by learning to start focusing on yourself.

Typically, when we want so much to help others and keep them safe, we focus only on them and ignore ourselves. We begin to bury our own feelings and needs. We harden ourselves to our own pain and suffering, and eventually our hearts begin to feel as if they're turning to stone, not unlike the hard, dull stucco coating of that Golden Buddha. We still feel, and feel deeply, but it becomes harder and harder to show and share those feelings.

In the process of trying to help others, too often, we become the casualties. More than one-third of COs say that someone in their life has told them that, since becoming a CO, they've become more anxious and depressed. When we're unable to access care and tenderness for ourselves, we also lose the ability to be tender and caring toward our loved ones, and so we unintentionally hurt them. According to a survey examining the stress experienced by COs, fifteen percent reported having mood swings while more than eight percent said they experienced a total loss of feeling for their family and friends at least once a week. That's not what you signed on for when you became a CO, and it's not how you have to experience your life.

Distancing ourselves from our feelings is a protective mechanism, and like all protective mechanisms, it probably served an important at one time. Now, however, that same protective mechanism has created a *dysfunction*. It's started to hurt instead of help. The insights, stories, and practices in this book will help release some of the tremendous pressure you are feeling so that you can reconnect with your true nature and the power of love inside you. Connecting with the power of love is not about becoming weak or ineffective; in fact, it is the opposite. Love allows us to see and speak truth, and to connect with the truth in others. Love is the energy of life, and we can learn to wield it like a sword to pierce even the toughest exterior.

Transformation is not easy. The ancient Celts had a process for breaking open stone. They would start a roaring fire and put the stone inside it, stoking the fire until the stone was burning hot. Then they would toss cold water on the stone. The sudden temperature change would cause the stone to crack open. As the poet Rumi wrote, "You have to keep breaking your heart until it opens." Soulmaking is hard work, and sometimes painful. But it's worthwhile, and you don't have to make the journey alone.

The Path of Soulmaking

Making a soul is like building a home. It's your true home, one that can never be burned down or foreclosed on. When constructing any home, there's a series of steps to follow and an order in which to follow them. Those steps and that order are contained in this book. The building, you must do yourself. Again, it's the labor of a lifetime, so it's best to approach it as a labor of love.

We'll begin with a plan, a blueprint, for what you're building. We'll start with the options in front of you at the point when you must make a choice. And we'll delve into what it means to embody your genius or your calling, and what that might look like for you.

Next comes the clearing of the ground. The excavation. You'll start by understanding and accepting that you're worth this mighty effort, that your gifts are very real, and that, given time, attention, and nurturing, they will reveal themselves. You'll acknowledge your past experiences and the projections people have put on you. You'll examine the toll that trauma has taken in your life—both your own, and the trauma experienced by those in your care. And we'll discuss how you can clear the way for a solid foundation.

The third step is pouring the foundation to create a solid base. We'll look at how you can learn to do something that will probably feel unnatural for you—putting yourself before others. Though caring for yourself first is a concept that's probably hard to grasp given your deep desire to care for and protect others, you'll see why it's a crucial component of your ability to fulfill your purpose effectively and over the long term. You'll also examine the survey map of your land, making note of its borders, and learning how boundary violations affect you and those around you.

Then it will be time for construction—building your house. This will involve opening your mind to a concept and system of order that's different from the one you've known—because the last thing you want to do is mindlessly recreate the previous structure. It may have done its job, sheltering you in the past, but now it's time for something different, something more. To do this, you'll consider new ways of relating to yourself and others. And, of course, you can't build without the necessary tools. You'll learn new ways to communicate and discover the power of *flow*—what it is and how to experience it more often in your work and your life.

It would be great if your work were done once construction was finished, but as any home-dweller knows, there's always maintenance. Once we sit down in our comfy chair and survey what we've created, we quickly start to notice that we could improve upon the work we've already done. As the journey of this book comes to a close, you'll create a plan for continuing your work, for realizing the full depth and breadth of your transformation, and for experiencing the pleasure and satisfaction of living your purpose.

Dealing with Initial Discomfort

Right now, thinking about such a huge undertaking, you might be experiencing anxiety, fear, excitement, or a mixture of all the above. Know that at the most basic level, these feelings are your brain signaling to you through chemical and electrical messengers: *I'm about to be challenged. I'm about to explore new territory.* When we approach a challenge, whether it's learning something new, starting an exercise program, or developing a new thought pattern, our brain releases a combination of electrical signals and chemical transmitters, including *norepinephrine*—the brain's version of adrenaline. These chemical messengers can make our minds and bodies feel agitated or anxious, unleashing sensations that we might experience as unpleasant and, therefore, negative. But what these chemicals and signals are doing is helping you to focus, and enabling your brain to change. They are preparing for your transformation.

As you go through this process, you will literally become a new person—the version who's been inside you, waiting to come out. Your brain and your body will help you by making new connections and bringing to life parts of yourself that have been ignored or shut down, starting on the cellular level and rippling outward, shifting your perspective and your feelings.

How you engage with life will change.

You'll feel more effective and connected.

You'll embody that superhero who has always been alive inside you.

Meaningful change is hard at first. Imagine crossing a field after a blizzard. There's no path in sight, and it's hard to make your way through waist-deep snow. But as you travel the trail more often, following in your own footprints, a route is carved, and it becomes easier to make your way.

It all begins with one step.

Followed by another.

Then another.

And before you know it, you are home.

"When I was in my mid-thirties, I had worked different jobs, but I was searching for something that would give me more of a sense of purpose. I had an opportunity to move to Kansas for a job with the Department of Corrections in Ellsworth. I just loved it. I found this family, this home, where I could... use my gifts of humor and my ability to teach in different ways. I saw it as a new challenge."

~Gregory Piper, a CO who has served as a Master Key Control Sergeant, member of a Special Operations Response Team, Corrections Counselor, among other roles

THE CHOICE POINT

Explore the concept of choice and its profound impact on your wellbeing. Learn how your core beliefs shape your perceptions and reactions to situations.

Whether it was your first, fourth, fourteenth, or fortieth shift, most COs report having at least one that started, or ended, with some form of the question, *What have I gotten myself into?* Michelle Threatt, a 15-year veteran of Corrections, recalls this feeling. "The first day I walked into those gates and they shut behind me, I looked around at all of the inmates in their uniforms and the fear just hit me. ... The first inmate to ever speak to me walked up and said, 'Officer, what's your name?' I told him and he said, 'Tomorrow when you come in here, you show no fear. Because it's all over you.'" Yet just a few years after that terrifying first shift, Michelle was up for an award for Detention Deputy of the Year. Not only had she saved a prison resident from choking, she also survived a terrifying incident where someone who was admitted to the hospital ward managed to work loose a sink faucet and savagely beat Michelle over the head with it before trying to escape. In spite of her injuries, Michelle took off down the hall after him and, when given the opportunity to shoot him, held her fire. She had the option and the opportunity to retaliate, yet she chose not to. Instead, the prison resident was recaptured safely.

How is it that some COs love their job, while given the same circumstances, others hate it? That while some COs are despised by prison residents, others are respected and even revered? Why do some COs see their job as just a way to get paid, or worse, as an opportunity for abuse, while others hold a sense of honor and dedication around their work? How does a Greg become a Greg, and a Michelle become a Michelle?

It begins with perhaps the most powerful tool each of us wields—choice. In this chapter, we start the journey of soulmaking at the very beginning. At the choice point.

The Fundamental Choice

Every day you are surrounded by the consequences of choice. You see lives that, in some cases, in just the blink of an eye have been transformed by the impact of choice. To lie or not. To rape or not. To kill or not.

The reality is that every day each of us is faced with countless choices. When will we wake up? What will we eat? How will we conduct ourselves? The list is endless.

What if we were to tell you that at the heart of everything, at the very center of life, each of us faces a *single* choice? A choice so pivotal and influential that it shapes all of our other choices in life. And that this choice is the same for each and every one of us, regardless of our gender, the color of our skin, our incarceration status, and on. This choice relates to how we will meet life and all that it has to offer us. It is also a choice that, if we do not make it consciously, will be made by default, and not to our benefit.

Will I be a victim, or will I choose awareness?

When you encounter discomfort, pain, or other challenges, will you choose to avoid them, or to sit with these difficult sensations? Will you choose to experience life as what happens to you, or will you choose to see your role in all that is? Will you view everything that happens, your circumstances, what's given to you and what's withheld, as opportunities, as raw materials with which you can build your soul? Will you choose to try to exert control over the world around you, either through aggressive or passive means, or will you change the game, agreeing instead to take on the mantle of responsibility for your own life and all that comes with it? To understand and embrace that you are the shaper of your own outcomes? Will you opt to step out of the light-filled world of logic and certainty, and instead make the dark journey into something deeper, more lasting, and more real, even though the way is not always clear? And will you choose to welcome everyone around you, even incarcerated individuals, *especially* incarcerated individuals, as potential teachers who can provide profound insights for your own development?

When we experience any form of pain, for most of us our natural reaction is to try to make it stop. We need to react, often wildly, or do anything else that will expel the source of pain from our lives. With the incarcerated individuals we encounter, we tend to want them to shut up, to settle down, to obey. Their acting-out and their wrestling with their own challenges frustrates or angers us or fills us with fear. But discomfort isn't about what anyone else is doing. It is about your internal state—how you are *experiencing* what is happening.

A victim reacts to what is happening outside them. Someone who has chosen accountability is able to direct whatever energy is present in a situation in constructive ways. Think about martial artist Bruce Lee, who had what many regard as superhuman abilities. In addition to being a legendary martial artist, Lee was also a philosopher. One of his most famous adages was to "be like water." Lee said, "Do not be assertive, but adjust to the object, and you shall find a way around or through it. ... If you put water into a cup, it becomes the cup. You put water into a bottle and it becomes the bottle. You put it in a teapot, it becomes the teapot. Now, water can flow or it can crash. Be water, my friend."

Trying to make sense of prison is like trying to stop the flow of water. In many ways, prison is a senseless place. Less than half of COs believe they are making a positive difference in the lives of the prison residents, or that when an individual is released from prison, they will be better prepared to function as a law-abiding citizen. The way many prisons in the U.S. function, with a focus on warehousing over rehabilitation, defies logic. There is no way for the brain to make sense of it. However, all is not lost, because even in the most illogical of environments, the soul can take what is available and make *meaning*. Water finds a way.

Even in the most degrading, demeaning environment, there is opportunity. The question is not, *Why?* That is a victim's

"Darkness is everything I do not know, cannot control, and am often afraid of. But that's just the beginner's definition. If I am a believer in God, then darkness is also where God dwells. God may also be frightening and uncontrollable and largely unknown to me, yet I decide to trust God anyway."

~BARBARA TAYLOR, THEOLOGIAN AND EPISCOPAL PRIEST

question. The question is, *What?* What can I make of this place that will serve me? That will make me stronger? That will make me more open and loving? That will make me more resilient? And on. The opportunities are endless when you change the way you view your circumstances.

We'll explore the fundamental choice and this idea of 'victim consciousness' more in a moment, but first, let's clarify what we mean by your soul. This is an essential understanding as your soul is the source of your blueprint for the place inside yourself you will come to call *home*. It is also the most powerful resource at your disposal for operating lovingly and effectively in a gritty, chaotic, and nonsensical world.

What is Your Soul?

In this book, we'll refer to divinity as well as to God. This isn't meant to imply any particular interpretation of God, other than the energy that runs through all things, weaving us all together in a vast interconnected web. You can think of God as an organizing principle, as a Higher Power, Unity, or even as a Great Mystery. You can think of God simply as Love or as Home. This book is secular—it has no grounding in any religion or single concept of God. You are free to interpret God in a way that feels right and makes sense to you. But make no mistake—soulmaking requires that you believe in something larger than you. That some principle or force with more intelligence or insight decides your worth and your value. In this work, as you connect with your soul and remember your deepest self, your worthiness is not up for negotiation. That decision has already been made. As one of our friends says when it comes to her sense of her own worthiness, "That decision is above my paygrade." It's nonnegotiable.

As with God, the words *spirit* and *soul* are often associated with religion, but in their deepest truth they operate entirely free of such structures. As with God, you can choose to view them through the lens of a particular religion if that's helpful for you, but you don't have to.

The spirit is that inside you which aligns with logic and reason. The spirit is clean and crisp. It likes order and organization. Most formal religions are concerned with tending the spirit, and they lay down a prescribed series of steps and rules to follow to feel the unity of our spirit with God. Through our spirit, we carry the DNA of God inside us. This is powerful and beautiful. And it is not the soul. In many ways, we can think of the soul as the opposite. Not as anti-God, but as the seat of our self rather than our divinity.

It's tough to offer a precise definition of the soul, because by its very nature it is a messy entity, and not easily conceived of. It must be felt. Experienced. And it is as unique to you as your fingerprint. The soul is unkempt. It does not fear mud or grime. It thrives in chaos because it embraces any situation that requires us to grow. And it likes to lurk in dark places. Your soul drew you to your work as a CO, and it thrives in this unpredictable environment, ripe as it is with so much potential not just for chaos, but also for human flourishing, as the two often go together. Sometimes the soul comes up behind us and whispers in our ears, beckoning us to do things that we do not at first understand, and may never fully grasp with our logical minds. *Why would I choose this job even though I could probably find something easier, that would require less of me? Why would I offer that man a kind word when he's in prison for rape? Why would I opt not to punish a prison resident harshly for his insults, even though it's in my power to do so, and many even want and expect me to?*

The soul's urgings can come to us as unbidden and nonsensical thoughts, or we can feel its direction in wordless spaces within our bodies, inside our very cells. It speaks to us in myths and riddles, through fables, poetry, and art. To hear the soul, we must engage all of our senses. To receive its guidance, we must soften our gaze and cock our heads a bit to the side and allow ourselves to perceive things that are just out of focus. To comprehend its deep desires, we must allow ourselves to feel everything and deny nothing.

If that is frightening or unappealing, then you're paying attention. The path of soulmaking is not the path of complacence.

Like any relationship worth having, it will require your full attention and engagement.

Your soul asks much, and it gives much.

In our culture, we thrive on control, or rather the illusion of control, but control is impossible. Life cannot be tamed. When we're connected to our soul, though, we no longer need to control because we have the ability to respond and work with whatever arises. We "rise to the level of our training," as they say in the military. What we've trained is the ability to be centered in all situations—to know and respond from our deepest self, and in a way that is true and authentic to us.

As Richard Lovelace, a 17th century poet who was imprisoned for fighting on the side of the king during the English Civil War, wrote, "Stone walls do not a Prison make; Nor Iron bars a Cage... If I have freedom in my Love, And in my soul am free, Angels alone that soar above, Enjoy such Liberty." This is the space the soulmaker inhabits—the space where you create your own reality through the choices you make about how you will interact with the world around you.

You and your fellow COs have quite a bit in common with those in your care. Every day you are surrounded by confinement. By oppression and suppression. You see broken bodies, broken spirits, and wounded souls. In some ways, the only difference is that you get to sleep on a real mattress, eat a pizza if you want, and get a week off every year. Other than that, though, you're constantly exposed to the same brand of stress, violence, and despair.

Yet every once in a while, there is someone different. Someone who enjoys liberty in spite of their circumstances, and in some ways, they find a greater freedom inside themselves because of their harsh surroundings. A CO or an incarcerated individual who does not allow their external circumstances to master them, but instead has learned to master their circumstances. There is a Greg, a Michelle, or a Damien Echols.

Damien Echols was part of the infamous West Memphis Three—a group of teens who in 1994 were convicted in Arkansas of murdering three eight-year-old boys. Echols was sentenced

"It's how you see it. What really for me was a changing point was looking for the good that could come out of my bad situation. I purposely looked for it, and I molded that thing until I could see it—pitbull focus—and now, you know what, I'm living it."

~JAMILA DAVIS, AMERICAN AUTHOR, ACTIVIST, AND FORMER FEDERAL PRISONER #59253-053 to death and lived on death row, including 10 years in solitary confinement, for 18 years. Eventually he and his friends were released as part of a plea deal in which they were allowed to maintain their innocence, yet the state did not have to exonerate them. Echols described how he survived the hopeless circumstances he experienced each day by doing what he could to reconnect with his soul and embrace its guidance, and that it all began with a single choice.

As Echols recalls, "The first guy I met in prison told me I could sit in my cell and slowly stagnate and go insane like the vast majority of the people in solitary *or* I could turn my cell into a monastery and continue to grow, evolve, and learn." He chose the latter. Even though, in many ways, Echols experienced some of the worst victimization many of us can imagine—first through his conviction then through his experiences in prison, where he says he was beaten and harassed repeatedly and mercilessly, including by COs—he chose to develop the consciousness of acceptance and accountability. He chose the path of soulmaking.

Owning and Harnessing Our Drive

One way we can frame this choice of victimhood versus accountability is whether we choose to operate in the land of projections, where our perceptions are based on unconscious beliefs, or we choose to see the truth and harness the power of our own inner workings. Philosopher Ken Wilber provides an instructive example.

Let's say you want to clean out your garage. It's a total mess, filled with things you know you'll probably never use again, and so cluttered you have trouble finding the things you're actually looking for. One Saturday morning you get up bright and early, put on some old clothes, pour a fresh cup of coffee, and head out to the garage. At this point, explains Wilber, you're in touch with your drive. Maybe you're not relishing the work ahead of you, but you're focused more on your desire to have a clean garage than you are on the drudgery of the work ahead.

When you open the garage door and survey the task, however, something starts to shift. *Man, there's a lot of stuff. How did all this crap wind up in here, anyway?* Instead of getting down to business, you come upon some abandoned projects and start to tinker a bit. You move a box here, shift one there, but without making any real progress. At this stage, you're still in contact with your drive to have a clean garage, but that connection has faded a bit. You're starting to forget it, and as Wilber explains, that's when you'll start to *alienate* it, or see it as something outside of you.

Your drive is still active, so it demands attention, but you're less aware of it. You don't feel *your* desire to clean the garage as much as *a* desire to clean the garage. It exists, but you don't recognize it as belonging to you. So, feeling this drive to clean the garage but not identifying with it, you start to get annoyed, tossing things around. Who's making you do this, anyway? It's a gorgeous day. There are so many other things you could be doing, and after all, you only have so much time off work. You should be relaxing! At this point, a projection exists, but it's without direction. Like a heat-seeking missile, it's zooming around, looking for a target.

Enter, your spouse, who peeks in and asks, "Hey, how's it going?"

Target: acquired. Now you're free to project your irritation on your spouse, perceiving that they are the source of the drive to clean the garage.

"Geez," you reply, "I said I'd do it and I'll do I it—stop nagging me!"

Now you might believe it was your spouse's drive that's got you shut up in the garage on a gorgeous Saturday morning. But if you were truly disconnected with the drive to clean the garage—if it belonged to your spouse alone, and you decided it was more important for you to get some rest that day instead of clean, you could simply have said, "You know, honey, I was thinking I'd do this today, but I really had a rough week and I could use some recovery time, and it's such a beautiful day. How about if we take a nice walk, instead?" But you don't do that because you are connected to the drive. It matters to you. But since you're not aware of the connection, and since *someone* wants the garage to be cleaned, it must be your spouse.

Another way to perceive of a projected drive is as *pressure*. When we feel pressure, we feel a projected drive coming at us from the outside. That heat-seeking missile has locked its sights back on us, but we have no idea that we're the ones who launched the missile to begin with.

Let's look at this idea of drives and projection from the standpoint of your work. One of the reasons your work can feel so stressful is because you have a drive to help people who are incarcerated be in some way rehabilitated or otherwise experience a positive change because of their time in prison. You know that even though you can't totally affect the outcome, you do play a role in how that situation unfolds. If you didn't have a drive for this result to occur, you wouldn't care what happened to the prison residents. When it feels like the odds are stacked against you in your work, when it feels like the challenge is overwhelming, you can start to externalize that drive and project it on those around you. You feel pressure from your coworkers, or your boss, or the prison residents themselves.

When we externalize our drives, we are choosing to meet the world as victims. We feel powerless over the forces acting upon us, and we become aggressive to what we perceive as pressure from others, or we push back on them, yelling, using abusive language, or even physical force. Or we become passive. We turn down the volume on our frustration and our feelings by shutting down our emotions or drowning them in anything that can help us tune them out, whether it's alcohol, food, television, or drugs.

The alternative and the way of accountability is to recognize that if we feel pressure, then the drive must come from within us. And if we can connect with that drive, we can act on it. We can find constructive ways to interact with prison residents which can support their rehabilitative process. We can develop tools for interaction that demonstrate love and compassion, providing them with an atmosphere in which change is not only possible, but more likely.

As Damien Echols wrote in his journal during prison, "I believe love can fix anything...I just need more of it than I can get in here." We can make that transformative love readily available.

Our level of awareness about our drives and projections has a massive impact on how we experience life. Similarly, our thoughts are powerful shapers of our life experience, and of the experiences of those around us.

Our Core Beliefs

Some of the thoughts we have seem transient—they are situational and rely on what's happening around us at the moment. Other thoughts have been around much longer and play in the background of our lives like a movie soundtrack. Many of these thoughts, which we call *core beliefs*, were inherited from our family members. As very young children, from our earliest days, based on the actions and inactions, the words, the responses, the tone of voice, the presence or lack of affection from others, we developed core beliefs about *the way life is*. These beliefs function as unquestioned assumptions. *People who've done bad things are bad people, and they'll never change.* Or, *Given the right circumstances, anyone could make destructive choices. Love has the power to open any heart.*

Chamelle experienced a shift in her core beliefs when she chose to relate to her role as a CO not as a victim, but as a someone who is in touch with and accountable for her drives and motivations. She explains, "I had this big 'a-ha' moment and realized I didn't have to be mean. I didn't have to go cold. They are inmates, but at the end of the day, they are also human beings. One could be my brother or my sister. It could even be me in there. When I started changing the way I acted toward them and my perception of them, my job got easier, and it shifted my whole perspective." Rather than living life as a victim, operating in reaction to what others do or don't do, Chamelle recognized herself as the shaper of her own experiences. With that, she was able to see the power and potential of the impact she can have on others when she operates in conscious collaboration with this creative energy of life.

Negative core beliefs, such as Chamelle's original belief that the individuals she worked with were inhuman and otherwise fundamentally different from her, operate like a tape playing in the background so quietly that we often aren't aware of it. Yet these beliefs shape our conscious thoughts and actions. We allow these unquestioned assumptions to define us and our world.

When we do not make an active choice to engage with life not just thoughtfully, but soulfully, our reality is controlled by our external circumstances. We are at the whim of what's going on in the outside world, with little to no ability to control our internal state. Instead, our lives become a reaction, and any goals or desires we want to realize or experience are held hostage by what happens around us. We cannot direct our lives. Victim consciousness is everywhere, because it is the choice that is made by default, when we do not consciously choose to experience life otherwise.

What does *otherwise* look like? In a word: freedom.

It is the choice to see everything life gives you, from the love of your partner to the anger and hatred of those you work with (or vice versa), as an opportunity for growth, for understanding, for learning. It is to live without judgment of your circumstances and to accept what is. To dedicate yourself to seeking out what is true in this moment and separating it from what is not—the unconscious thought patterns, including projections, that would lead you back to victim consciousness. When we operate as a victim, we tense and push back. We try to force some concept of external justice or logic onto a situation. Instead of letting it be what it is, we try to force a narrative fueled by our unconscious core beliefs.

As Bruce Lee observes, "If nothing within you stays rigid, outward things will disclose themselves." When we tense and shift into victim mode, we become blind to what is possible. If we stay open and pliable, willing to work with what is, endless possibilities become available to us.

Remember Michelle, who experienced a vicious assault? She was truly victimized in that experience and at first, she did wonder, *Why me?* But as she now says, "My question now is, 'Why not me?' I'm glad it was me because that seed [my attacker] planted pushed me into my purpose. I still call it the 'best worst day of my life' because everything changed for the better." This is the power of accountability. It is an agreement to live in perpetual flow with all that is—to do as Bruce Lee says and be like water.

How Opening to Struggle Makes Us Stronger

Scientists who study the brain say that people who are able to meet life on their own terms, rather than meet it with fear or unnecessary aggression or by freezing and shutting down, who instead cultivate a willingness to lean into their discomfort and who say "yes" to circumstances, are those who most consistently raise their level of performance. *They do life better.* They are more resilient and recover more quickly. They continually expand what they're capable of, physically, emotionally, and on, because with each incidence in which they lean in willingly, their ability to perform well in challenging circumstances grows. In a very real way, they become unlimited.

Similarly, scientists are now looking at stress differently. We're mostly taught that stress is bad, and when it's chronic, it's true that it can have some extremely negative effects. But not all stress is bad.

One psychologist, Kelly McGonigal, who is an expert in stress research, describes stress simply as a signal that we're meant to move. For example, the body releases stress hormones early in the morning that make you hungry and thirsty. The stress is designed to get you to move so that you take care of your body's needs. That's a good thing. The stress of loneliness, as McGonigal describes it, feels terrible, but its underlying message is that it's moving you to connect with others. We know human relationships are essential for our health and wellbeing, so this is another example of stress actually serving us. As McGonigal says, "Embracing stress is more important than reducing stress."

So, we're not just trying to cut off all of our stress signals or live in some kind of perpetually happy space where we become disconnected from ourselves. Instead, we're becoming smarter and more thoughtful of the signals around and inside us, becoming better judges of how we're meant to move in the world that creates the most benefit for ourselves and others.

Those who learn to lean in to challenges are people who, when a battle presents itself, draw their swords and run toward it. The battle is often metaphoric, but sometimes—especially for you—it may be quite literal. These are the guards who are able to deal with prison residents' defensive and aggressive behaviors and with other challenging circumstances without internalizing the experience—reliving the stress in an unending loop—or numbing their emotions.

Seeing people locked up for months and years on end, seeing so many lives lived in confinement, has the potential to be soul crushing. If you are dealing with these and other horrors of your work by shutting down your feelings, you've likely found that it's not so easy to turn them back on again when you clock out and go home. When you teach yourself to become numb to circumstances that evoke a difficult emotional response, it's like throwing the master switch on an electrical box. The power to everything—the ability to really feel anything—is switched off.

Ben King served in the Iraq War as a Psychological Operations Sergeant. He says it was nearly a decade before he realized the deep psychological effects his deployment had on him. As a result of his experiences and his struggle to deal with trauma, King created Armor Down, an organization that helps service members and others who have learned to "armor up" as a way to cope with their work, compartmentalizing and shutting down their feelings, learn instead how to "armor down." King explains it's not about feeling perpetual peace or losing your edge, it's about learning how to engage *all* of your resources more effectively and appropriately all day, every day. When you live from a standpoint of acceptance and accountability, King says, "You can recognize when you're getting spun up and instead of getting into flat-out aggressor mode, you can get into a space of being able to assess the situation with your highest level of processing and perceiving. It's not that conflict disappears, it's that whatever shows up is no longer 'good' or 'bad.' There's no longer that narrative. You look instead at the qualities that show up and your relationship to them. You observe how you can participate with an incident of aggression, for example, in a way that affords you the opportunity to control the situation without getting attached to it."

You never have to turn off your feelings. Instead, you relate to them differently, using them to inform your actions.

Anyone who is consistently exposed to harsh realities benefits from this ability to retain flexibility in how we relate with life. Every day, Mother Teresa was exposed to massive amounts of human suffering in the rank, dirty slums of Calcutta. Much of the suffering she saw, she could do little to nothing to alleviate. Yet she was not consumed by it, nor did she have to shut down her feelings to cope with it every day. Over decades of service, she was able to help countless people—thousands upon thousands. This same woman, who lived with the horrifying consequences of human neglect and uncaring, once said: "If you judge people, you have no time to love them." Instead of focusing on judging those who could have helped but didn't, she focused on the power of love to impact the lives of everyone around her. She did not let what was around her every day make her jaded or numb; she opened to it, and she was able to do this because of her deep connection to her soul. One thing you never see said or written about Mother Teresa is that she was weak or ineffective.

When we learn to move toward our circumstances, no matter how daunting, we are able to maintain our center. If force of some kind is required, we are able to apply it appropriately. We are able to maintain balance, feeling that steady center point inside us. This center is our soul. Your soul will become the truth to which you orient as you interact with life, because nothing and no one knows you better. Simply being who you are and remaining rooted in yourself will begin to influence your surroundings. All that is around you will relate to you differently, and you to it, simply because of the way you walk in the world.

Who We Are Affects Others

Scientists study an almost mystical, but very real phenomenon called *limbic resonance*. We're aware of the idea that babies can't self-regulate most of their own internal processes. You've probably seen a toddler just starting to walk take a few tentative steps, then fall. Immediately she looks to her mother. Based on how her mother responds, whether she expresses distress that the baby has fallen, or whether she offers a smile and a gentle "oops!", the baby responds by crying or by laughing and getting back up. She is reading her mother for cues as to how she should feel. Similarly, when a baby cries and her mother picks her up and holds her close, offering soothing sounds and rubbing her back, this interaction helps to regulate the baby's nervous system and calm her. We share deep emotional states with one another through limbic resonance—the limbic, or emotional, centers of our brains, actually signal one another. And this doesn't only happen in childhood, but throughout our whole lives. Though eventually our bodies learn to self-regulate in many ways, we still pick up a tremendous number of cues from other people. If you've ever heard the idea that emotions are contagious, it's because of limbic resonance. As poet John Donne observed, no man is an island. What one of us does and what one of us feels impacts us all.

You experience this every time you are in the presence of people whose minds and hearts are filled with anger and aggression and you begin to feel irritated and disgruntled, or when you come home and your dog jumps up into your lap and you begin to pet him and feel a sense of calm settle over you. You've likely noticed how prison residents and Correctional Officers affect one another, pulling each other up or down. You've seen this among your coworkers, too, if you've ever had that toxic person on your team or your shift who seems to pollute the very air around them with their negativity.

Most of this influence is unconscious. It's like some invisible force is driving our train.

Later in this book, we will discuss the importance of connecting with our emotions and bodily states, along with our thoughts, so that we can *consciously* drive our train. We become aware of our direction and of all obstacles in our path, and we are able to seamlessly course-correct when necessary.

When you choose the soul path, you commit to consciously driving your own train. When this happens, you will become an unstoppable force, influencing everything and everyone around you. That does not mean you become responsible for others—in soulmaking you are responsible for yourself, alone. But you are responsible entirely, without excuse, without fail. Still, all you need to do is your best, then you can let go of the outcome, for yourself and others. That will take care of itself. People in your life—your family, your coworkers, the incarcerated individuals you watch—they are responsible for their own souls. They will be influenced by you. What they do with that influence is up to them. That is their choice.

> *"It is never easy to demand the most from ourselves, from our lives, from our work. To go beyond the encouraged mediocrity of the society we live in is always fraught with danger and with fear."*
>
> ~AUDRE LORDE

The Challenge of Soulmaking

As we mentioned in the Introduction, the work of soulmaking is not easy. This choice may feel like a simple one and in many ways, it is, but it is a difficult one to make real in your life. In a society where people are encouraged toward passivity and on overreliance on faceless and soulless systems, blame and entitlement are the currency of the land. They are intoxicating and can be extremely difficult to give up. It's easy to blame the system. It's easy to blame the prison residents. There are very real problems in your work, very real challenges. But in time and with practice, you will become accustomed to a different reality, one where you experience true control—not over your circumstances, but over your reactions to circumstances. You will begin to master your inner world and see from this vantage point that the only power others have over you is that which you willingly give them.

Chamelle describes her own realization. "I have to say, I did not like my job for the first ten years, but I needed it for the great benefits and decent pay. The first two and a half years in High Point, my job was hard and intense, but I learned that I was the one that made my job so hard. It wasn't the inmates. It was me..."

In this world of soulmaking, the most difficult battles are reserved for those who are strongest. Think of them—of yourself—as a member of the soul's Special Forces. The tip of the spear. This choice, the choice for absolute presence and absolute accountability, is one most people do not make. By stepping on this path, you go where others dare not tread. (The fact that you opted for a career as a CO shows that you are already willing to take the brave, noble, and unconventional path.) Your life will change dramatically as a result of this choice. As you grow into yourself and you meet life differently, you will no longer settle for the mediocre. You will no longer settle for numbness, even when feeling and full presence brings you pain. You will be willing to feel the pain so that you can also feel the exquisite joy of aliveness. And you will learn that pain is like fertile soil in which you can grow and harvest many things.

Make no mistake, the battles will continue. Life will not suddenly become easy. But like Neo in *The Matrix* films, you will learn to read the code behind the illusions and the temptations to blame others that present themselves so that you can interact with life purposefully and powerfully, on your own terms. You will not become bulletproof in the sense that nothing will ever hurt you again, because truly being alive necessitates feeling everything. You will experience wounding, and you will bear scars, but like Michelle, those scars will represent aspects of newfound strength and deeper understanding. You will see them as evidence of a life lived well and richly, as a map of where you have been and all you have learned.

Now, here, is where you decide what home you will build. Where you begin to connect with your soul and begin to remember its blueprint. It, along with everything else in this world, begins with a choice: *Who will I be in this moment, and in every moment that follows?*

Integration Exercises

- What do you believe to be true about life?

- What about life scares you?

- What is imprisoned in you? Concealed? Locked away? What pieces of you feel like they should be kept hidden away because they are not fit for "polite society"?

- Do you ever feel numb, like you have trouble connecting to your emotions? When do you notice this?

- Can you recall an experience or moment in your life when you felt truly free? When was it? What did it feel like in your body, sound like, smell like? (If you are struggling to connect with bodily sensations, don't worry—if you've learned to numb sensations, it can take time to reconnect with them, but in time you will.)

- Do you ever overreact or otherwise react inappropriately to circumstances? Do you notice any patterns related to when this occurs?

"Being a CO is hard. Many people can't handle that job. My brother has been a street cop for 23 years and has faced many dangers, but he said that he wouldn't work in a prison. I think it takes a special person to get locked behind the walls, outnumbered one hundred to one with no weapon."

~Gary York, an Army veteran who served nearly 29 years as a CO in the Florida State prison system

RECOGNIZING WHAT WANTS TO MOVE THROUGH YOU

See the role that different archetypes play in your life. Embrace your archetypes to achieve personal fulfillment and a sense of purpose in your work.

We've now addressed the fundamental choice point—whether to assume a victim mindset or to embrace full accountability, accepting your role in all that is present in your life. We've also acknowledged the vision—a world in which prisons are more like monasteries, spaces that support the work of soulmaking. Yet in order for this to be possible, the monks need guides. They need for you to act as a mentor and protector. This isn't a favor you're doing them; the relationship you have with those in prison is symbiotic. By acting as monks, those you care for will *make* you into mentors and protectors. In this lesson, though, we will explore the actual forces within you that will support you to fully realize your role as a Guardian.

As Gary said in the quote above, it does take a special person to be a CO, a person with the motivation to not only help others, but to be willing to put themselves in harm's way to do it. There's a powerful energy around your work that moves from inside you, a force that compels you to run toward the alarm bells while others would run away. That has you willing to enter high-pressure situations again and again because of your commitment to your work and to those you serve. But how do you become this person? What is within you, about you, that makes you unique in this way?

What determines who we are at our core is more than just a genetic lottery, or the sum of our experiences as children. Operating underneath it all are invisible patterns that pull on us, tugging, yanking, coaxing us to embody all that is within us. They are our *archetypes*.

The Nature of Archetypes

As you've no doubt seen in life, there are warriors and there are Warriors. There are mothers and there are Mothers. There are teachers and there are Teachers. There are those who merely fill a role, and there are those who fulfill it. They don't just have a job or play a part; they live a calling. This calling is an archetypal pattern.

You're no doubt familiar with some mythology: larger than life stories of magic and mystery, tragedy and triumph. They give us a language in which we can express and interpret our experiences. Today, we often equate the word *myth* with something that is false. But something that is "made up" is simply a creation, in the way we might throw a piece of pottery or build a woodshed.

You've probably had the experience of reading a novel or seeing a movie where you felt deeply moved. Even though the story was fictional, it connected with something inside you. You experienced an emotional resonance with the characters, or maybe one character in particular. Stories, fables, poetry, mythology... these are all containers we have created to make sense of our experiences, and to share those experiences and the realizations we've gained from them with one another. Those stories that survive the test of time do so because of their strong resonance, in how powerfully they tap into universal human experiences. Archetypes go hand in hand with mythology in that they are a way of relating to deep unseen forces at work in our lives. Like myths, they are a way of connecting with the dimension of the soul.

Professor and comparative mythologist Joseph Campbell described the "hero's journey," which is the common path of anyone who receives a calling (and then refuses that calling, but finally accepts it), faces a crisis and is victorious (or may face many crises), and then comes back home a changed person. One of the best-known ancient examples of the hero's journey is the hero Odysseus in Homer's epic poem, "The Odyssey." Yet the

"We are lived by powers we pretend to understand."

~W.H. AUDEN

hero's journey is also the journey of Luke Skywalker and countless other modern heroes. In fact, in some way, you could say that we're all called to the hero's journey. That journey may be a literal calling away from home involving actual travel, but it may also be an inner journey. A journey of soulmaking. A spiritual quest in which we engage with significant challenges and eventually return home to ourselves. The journey from Guard to Guardian is a such a journey.

The hero is an *archetype*, a word that essentially means an original pattern or prototype. The concept is ancient, and Greek philosopher Plato is acknowledged as the originator of the idea. When you think of a hero, immediately your mind conjures a series of people, whether real-world or fictional. Superman, Indiana Jones, Martin Luther King, Jr., a firefighter, a pilot who lands a disabled plane saving all the passengers. These people are quite different, yet all embody the archetype of the hero.

You can think of an archetype as a pattern that's embedded inside you and that influences you, even though you may be unaware of it or even actively deny it. Archetypes represent our callings to fulfill. They shape our perceptions and interactions with the world around us. They call to us, fueling and directing our deepest desires.

The principle of archetypes is so common that even corporations now use this language. The Hartford, an insurance company, says that each company's brand has an archetype, or a collection of unspoken characteristics that shape how the company connects with their customers. For example, a company with the hero archetype seeks to improve the world, is willing to endure adversity, and is courageous, bold, and honorable. Today, it's even common to see business leaders characterized as hero-leaders or servant-leaders—language that refers to archetypes. Psychologist Carl Jung said, "All the most powerful ideas in history go back to archetypes."

Whether we have the hero archetype or any number of others, engaging fully with our archetypes changes us. When we recognize the archetypes to which we're connected and we learn to embrace

"Whether you call someone a hero or a monster is all relative to where the focus of your consciousness may be."

~JOSEPH CAMPBELL

"I think I was meant to be in this field. It was fun growing up with my father being a Correctional Officer. I remember during the summer I'd go hang out at the jail. Sometimes I would stay the night, sleep on a cot in the back of the office, and just hang out and watch the inmates play basketball."

~STEVE MAYNARD, A CO WITH NEARLY 15 YEARS OF EXPERIENCE WHO NOW WORKS FOR GUARDIANRFID them, a sacred and spiritual transformation happens within us at the soul level. We become who we already are—what we describe as *remembering*. When we remain ignorant of our archetypes or actively resist them, we are resisting our true selves, the selves that long to come forward and be alive in us. In this state of resistance, it is impossible to experience eudaimonia, which is when we are fully flourishing. We spend so much energy denying and suppressing our true selves that we exhaust ourselves and block the life-force energy that yearns to move freely through us.

Russell Hamilton worked for nearly 30 years as a CO. Eventually, he was promoted to Sergeant, then figured it was time to retire, but the pull he felt to Corrections was too strong. "It didn't take very long to figure out retirement wasn't for me," said Russell. "I went back to work as a Senior Juvenile Correctional Officer at a brand-new facility. I now work for a company that specializes in rehabilitation and re-entry for people on probation, trying to get them to think differently about their life so that they change their ways."

You might think of archetypes like dark matter in space—you can't see them, but they exert a kind of gravity on you in a way that your life somehow organizes around them. We feel drawn to some things and not others. Someone with the Teacher archetype is compelled to teach, as someone with a Servant archetype is compelled to serve. Their path, regardless of the specific details, will always lead them in some way toward fulfilling these roles, whether as a career or otherwise. As the poet Rilke describes it, "...we are grasped by what we cannot grasp." Even though we cannot see or touch our archetypes, they are alive inside us.

Psychologist James Hillman describes archetypes as the "fundamental fantasies that animate all life." Hillman described archetypal patterns as *blueprints* embedded within us. He also described these patterns as our *acorn*, because the acorn carries inside it the imprint of the oak tree it is destined to become. When the acorn is nurtured, it takes root and grows automatically, without needing any force outside it to direct it. It knows inherently what it is meant to be.

French philosopher Henry Corbin described archetypes as part a field of imagination that all humans share. Archetypes live in this world of our imagination, yet it's a mutually created world. Like the hero's journey, archetypes are part of our collective experience of being human.

Like myths, just because something is imagined does not mean it is false or not a *real* creation. At one point, Harry Potter, hero of the book series, experiences a space inside (or perhaps outside) himself where he visits with his former headmaster, Professor Dumbledore, who has died. Harry asks Dumbledore if the place they are is real, or in his head, to which Dumbledore replies, "Of course it is happening inside your head, Harry, but why on Earth should that not mean it's real?" In fact, everything that eventually comes to be in "the real world" (like that pottery or that shed) first existed in someone's imagination. Just as right now, you are beginning to imagine living your work as a Guardian.

How We Live Our Archetypes

You can think of your archetypes as part of the essence of you, and you can live out that essence in many ways. Someone who has the Servant archetype, for example, isn't necessarily a police officer. They could be a doctor, mentor, or executive assistant. The Guardian, too, is a Servant archetype. Archetypes can also operate separate from vocation. You can be a baker, but connect with your Servant archetype by volunteering at a local food pantry. You can have the Teacher archetype, but work as a stockbroker who tutors his niece in mathematics on the weekends. What is consistent is that when we come into alignment with our blueprint, we actively integrate our archetypes into our lives in some way.

In the quote at the start of this chapter, Gary said that it takes a "special kind of person" to be a CO. That language signals an archetype. That's one of the reasons COs often feel a special bond with one another—not only do you share similar experiences, you also have in common a deep calling to do the work you do.

"The power of imagination makes us infinite."

~JOHN MUIR

"At the deepest level of the human heart, there is no simple, singular self. Deep within, there is a gallery of different selves. Each one of these figures expresses a different part of your nature."

~JOHN O'DONOHUE, ANAM CARA: A BOOK OF CELTIC WISDOM

Imagine someone has the Warrior archetype. This doesn't mean they've been in the military. What characterizes the Warrior archetype is deeper—it's a desire to protect the essence or the heart of others. In this way, Warriors are also seen as protecting their tribe, homeland, or nation. They are protecting the essence of those groups or structures. William Wallace, the real-life hero chronicled in the movie *Braveheart*, fought to preserve Scotland's independence, which was an essential part of the nation's identity.

An example of a real-life, modern-day Warrior is David Goggins. Goggins grew up with an exceptionally abusive father and as a result he suffered low self-esteem and performed poorly in school. He couldn't read, he stuttered, and on top of it, he had asthma. No one, especially Goggins himself, would have guessed him to have the Warrior as one of his archetypes. After dropping out of school, though, Goggins decided to join the Air Force, but was discharged because it was discovered that he had sickle cell trait and therefore could develop sickle cell anemia. Dejected, Goggins became morbidly obese as he worked a series of boring, unfulfilling jobs, including spending night shifts spraying empty restaurants for cockroaches.

One night after work, Goggins was sitting drinking a milkshake when he saw a television ad that showed young men his age training to be Navy SEALs. It looked like torture, but inside Goggins, something sat bolt upright. Suddenly, the idea of becoming a SEAL was a vision he couldn't shake, because it connected with the most formidable part of his being—the Warrior archetype inside him. Over and over, recruiters told Goggins he didn't have what it took. He was too dumb and too fat, they told him. Finally, one recruiter decided to give him a shot, telling Goggins he'd have to hit the books hard and lose 106 pounds, all in less than three months, but if he did it, he'd get a shot at becoming a SEAL. It was a massive effort, but because he knew that his goal, no matter how far-fetched it seemed to others, was in total alignment with who he was inside, Goggins committed himself completely. He managed to qualify for Basic Underwater Demolition/SEAL (BUD/S) training. During BUD/S, even though he made it through the infamous Hell Week, Goggins contracted pneumonia and was forced to quit. When he recovered, he started BUD/S again, but this time he experienced a fractured kneecap and was again forced to quit. Goggins returned a second time and finally completed BUD/S. He then went on to complete the Army's Ranger training and continued on to become an Air Force Tactical Controller—the first person ever to complete all three. After a 20-year military career, he became an ultra-athlete, competing in grueling 100+-mile sporting events to raise money for the families of fallen service members.

It's easy to see Goggins as a Warrior because he was in the armed forces, but look deeper and you'll see that this Warrior patterning emerged again and again in multiple ways in his life. First, he connected with this Warrior archetype to protect himself. His own essence, his soul, was drowning in the misery of an unfulfilling life until he fought to claim his true heart. During his training, Goggins became known as a source of inspiration to those around him, helping them connect with their essence and their heart. When he became an ultra-athlete, it was with the goal of raising money to support the families of fallen service members so that these people would have the financial support to pursue education and other avenues of exploration that honored their essence. And as a motivational speaker and writer, Goggins helps to show people a path through which they can recognize and actualize their own inner blueprints.

That is the power of an archetype—if you have it, you will feel its pull no matter what your life circumstances.

Archetypes and Congruence

If David Goggins had ignored that TV commercial for the Navy SEALs, if he'd have just finished his milkshake and gone to bed, his Warrior archetype would not have gone quiet. In fact, the energy of his archetype would have begun to work even harder to get his attention. Maybe his life would have become more miserable. Maybe his car would have broken down outside a Navy

"When you can get into an industry or a profession where you can possibly make a difference in somebody's life, that becomes part of your choice, and it certainly was for me."

~ANDY, VETERAN CO AND FOUNDER OF CO ORGANIZATION ONE VOICE UNITED recruiting center. Who knows? One thing is for certain—when we ignore our archetypes or they go unrecognized, the force they exert on us can range from uncomfortable and confusing to downright painful. We might question why things don't seem to be working or lining up in our lives, or why everything feels like such a struggle. We might be tempted into victim consciousness, thinking we don't deserve to struggle in this way. Yet our struggle isn't because something is wrong. Our struggle is our archetypes communicating with us that our lives lack *congruence*. That we're not living the life that is meant for us.

Another way to think about congruence is as *alignment*. Consider your spine. For most of us, our spine is made up of 24 bones. When they're lined up properly, our spine gives us structural support and helps us move. If you've ever experienced a back injury that causes one or more of these bones to twist or shift out of place, you know the extreme discomfort that can result. Not only do misalignments often cause physical pain, they can cause dysfunction. When your spine is misaligned, you can't have healthy posture, which in turn compresses your internal organs, certain movements become impossible, you can feel numbness and tingling throughout your body, and on. The misalignment of just one vertebra causes multiple challenges throughout your body.

The same thing can happen when we're out of alignment with our archetypes. We're working against the energies that want to be expressed through us, and that can be exhausting and painful, even if we're not conscious of what's going on. Think back to Lesson 1 and the relief and exhilaration Chamelle felt when she came into alignment with the Guardian archetype. It wasn't that her work as CO suddenly became easy, but suddenly things made sense. She understood a new way to relate to her work that was more effective and more meaningful, and that gave her greater ease. It relieved the stress and strain of the misalignment.

Each of us has a variety of archetypes that influence our psyche, some of which influence us more than others. They affect our drives, desires, and motivations, along with what gives us a sense of accomplishment and satisfaction. As we'll discuss in a moment, there are several archetypes that work together with the Guardian, contributing their unique gifts and skills to helping the Guardian realize its full essence.

Regardless of what our archetypes are, the same is true for all of us. Our work of soulmaking is not to focus on outcomes and goals, it is to focus on coming into alignment with ourselves. Recognizing our archetypes and how their energy wants to move through us is part of this alignment.

Archetypes don't work only on an individual level. Our archetypes also influence and are influenced by others' archetypes.

Archetypal Pairs

For every archetype you are connected to, others have complementary archetypes that connect and relate to those archetypes. These *archetypal pairs* work in relationship with one another. Mother and Child is one example. Archetypal pairs create a kind of balance of life energies.

Another example of a matched pair of archetypes is one that you in your role as a CO know a lot about: the Perpetrator and the Victim. These two archetypes are linked together because one creates and sustains the other.

In 1993, 16-year-old Oshea Israel shot and killed 20-year-old Laramiun Byrd. With this act, Israel came to embody the archetype of Perpetrator, and Mary Johnson, Byrd's mother, became the Victim. Understandably, Johnson hated Israel for what he had done, and this hatred reinforced their connection as Perpetrator and Victim. Then, however, something remarkable happened.

Years after her son's death, Johnson realized she wasn't the only one who had lost a son. Israel's parents had lost their son to incarceration. Johnson decided to form a support group for mothers who had lost children, whether they'd lost them to violence or to prison. Yet Johnson had a hurdle to overcome. She didn't think she would be able to relate to mothers of Perpetrators unless she attempted to forgive the Perpetrator who killed her own son. She reached out to Israel and asked if she could visit him and he agreed.

When the two saw each other, Israel asked if he could hug Johnson. "As I got up," she later told journalists, "I felt something rising from the soles of my feet and leaving me." She began to visit Israel regularly. When he was released after serving 15 years, Johnson approached her landlord and asked if he would overlook Israel's record and allow him to rent an apartment in her complex. The landlord agreed, and Johnson and Israel ended up as next-door neighbors.

Today, Johnson wears a double-sided locket with a picture of her son on one side and Israel on the other. Johnson and Israel visit churches and prisons, telling people their story and encouraging them to forgive. By acknowledging their archetypal connection and leaning into it rather than running from it, or viewing it as a source of unending pain, Johnson and Israel were able to shift from living in the negative aspects of these archetypes to realizing and embodying their positive and empowering aspects—to allowing the energy of these archetypes to move through them in a beneficial way.

Notice they didn't do this with the goal of changing others' lives, they did it to come into alignment with themselves. They each felt a call from their soul to do things that seemed wildly irrational—Johnson to ask to visit Israel and him asking to hug her; Johnson releasing her hatred of Israel, and Israel allowing himself to be loved. But by being who they are, listening to their souls and undertaking these actions that seem nonsensical to many of us, the natural result is that they have changed others' lives through their example. By allowing love to be present in their relationship, they created what we can think of as a field of love that, thanks to limbic resonance, everyone around them can experience, as well.

The Prisoner and the Guard/ian

Just as a Perpetrator creates a Victim, and a Victim identifies someone else as a Perpetrator, a Prisoner is inextricably linked to a Guard—the two are paired archetypes that have been intimately connected since time began. One could be in a literal prison, or they could be in a psychological prison, or both. The character Neo in *The Matrix* was in a literal *and* psychological prison until he chose to do the work of setting himself free. As part of the Unconditional Freedom Project, we are working with those who are in prison to connect with a deep sense of personal freedom, regardless of their surroundings.

In your experience as a CO, the Prisoner is someone who has been locked away to serve time for a crime. They have been deprived of freedom and an assortment of rights that those who are not or have never been imprisoned enjoy. As we mentioned in the last chapter, the Prisoner and the Guard also have much in common. The Prisoner spends most of their day inside walls of concrete. They often become hardened by the lack of love and compassion behind prison walls, and by a sense of having to constantly protect themselves. Yet underneath it all, neither of you have lost your humanity.

Jerome, who has more than a decade of experience as a CO, who has served as a Marine, and who has family in law enforcement, also has family who have been incarcerated. "One of my uncles who did seventeen years told me that, no matter what they've done, everyone is human. Don't look down on anybody. Don't worry about what they did. I have tried to follow that advice and be that type of Officer."

Luis Soto, a retired CO who now teaches classes in criminal justice, said, "Just because you're wearing a uniform doesn't mean the inmates are going to respect you. In fact, they're not going to respect you until you show respect for them." The Guardian recognizes the humanity of those in their care, and sees beyond labels to their innate worthiness and abilities.

As with all archetypes, there is an assortment of abilities common to the Prisoner that we would consider neither good nor bad—it's all in how they are applied. Movies and episodic shows depict the re-tasking of these kinds of skills and attributes. In the show *Leverage*, a group of former criminals (a so-called hitter, hacker, grifter, thief, and mastermind—sounds like a gang of archetypes, doesn't it?) work together to use their skills for good. The *Suicide Squad* movies and comics have a similar theme, with people characterized as villains being temporarily released from prison so they can save the world. In both cases, characters thought to be "bad guys" have a unique set of skills or attributes that they can use for positive or negative means. Think of the amount of influence a Guard has over a Prisoner's experiences. They can use this influence negatively, by berating and belittling a Prisoner, or positively, by providing support and encouragement.

CO Kyle says that among the prisoners in his care, it was common for them to self-harm. "I found that I was often able to talk them out of harming themselves. I'd get called in, I'd clear everyone out of the way and I'd say, 'Hey, dude, let's talk about it.' So, he'd know I was there to solve the problem, not to make it worse. He knew I was going to treat him with dignity and we were going to figure it out. I understood that we were not friends, but we could still talk man-to-man, because those inmates really just wanted somebody to listen to them, and nine times out of ten, that would be enough to talk them down. It may be that something specific happened, but in most cases, it's just the mental stress of being in prison that gets to them."

Some of the Prisoner archetype's skills can include survival intuition, adaptability, negotiation, strategic thinking, problem solving, indomitable will, and determination. You may have a few others to add that you've encountered in your work. Again, notice that none of these is inherently good or bad. They can each be tasked in service of the greater good, or toward more nefarious goals. They can be deployed in ways that are self-serving, or in ways that serve the Self.

The Guard keeps the Prisoner contained. The Guard ensures that the Prisoner serves their sentence and, if they're to be released, lives to see that day. By contrast, the Guardian archetype is tasked with much more. According to archetypal expert Susanna Barlow, people with the Guardian archetype seek to support others and want to feel that their work is of real value to those in need. They are happy to function as one part within a larger organization,

"Were it not for the leaping and twinkling of the soul, man would rot away in his greatest passion, idleness."

~CARL JUNG

but are happiest when they are respected for the invaluable services they perform. Guardians are loyal and protective. One of their superpowers is the ability to set aside their emotions in moments when clear and rational decision-making is required, especially when the stakes are high. Guardians are willing to put themselves in harm's way to protect others from someone who has the potential to cause great harm because of their actions, and to block someone from spaces where they don't belong.

Additionally, and powerfully, the Guardian sees the truth about the Prisoner—that regardless of what they may have done in their lives and the fact of their incarceration, their essence remains intact. Their true heart, their soul, and their blueprint remain unchanged. They see and embrace the Prisoner's worthiness, because in our essence, we all are worthy.

Yet for CO Brian, his day-to-day work experience was quite different. "When I first started, Officers had a say. If there was a classification hearing, when the inmate was going to be considered for lower security, they would bring us in and ask for our opinion. The same used to be true for disciplinary or parole hearings. Our opinions mattered. We don't do that anymore. We are just warehousing. I became jaded by the system when I realized we're not about correcting; we're about making sure they don't get out until they're supposed to. We hold them until their sentence is done and try to make sure that no one gets killed. When one inmate tries to kill another or injure another inmate, we get in the middle and stop it and usually neither one of them dies. Whether it's an assault, a medical emergency, a fire, or a riot we are the first, last, and only responders behind those walls."

In Brian's later experience, guards were not recognized for the significant value they can add to the prison environment. Instead, they were tasked with keeping prison residents detained and alive—that's all. It's not that these tasks are insignificant, it's that—as you know—COs are capable of much more. Just as the Prisoner has an array of qualities and skills that can be used thoughtfully and for great good, so too does the Guard.

"You have to ask, Where's the real problem? Is it the inmates? Or is it the job? It's the job. But that's good news, because that you can control. That you can change."

~BRIAN, LONGTIME CO
AND NATIONAL DIRECTOR
OF CO ORGANIZATION
ONE VOICE UNITED

When the Guard is able to connect with the full resources of their archetype, they become the Guardian, and they encourage and support the Prisoner in their own soulmaking task of becoming truly free. By invoking the essence-protecting qualities of the Warrior, the Guardian clears and holds space for the Prisoner to connect with their own heart, their true essence. By tending to the soul-based needs of the Prisoner, the Guardian also invokes the Servant archetype. It is only in the doing of this work that the Guard becomes the Guardian. In this way, working together, the Prisoner and the Guardian help one another realize their full potential.

The Gate

In ancient times, a daimon was thought of as a spirit assigned to be with us throughout our lives. Socrates described a daimon as a gift from God, or the gods. Psychologist Rollo May writes that the daimon, "is the urge in every being to affirm itself, assert itself, perpetuate and increase itself." The daimon is an energy that pushes and pulls us to engage with life fully and richly. We can think of daimonic energy as life-force energy, or as the energy of creation. It can be stressful, precisely because it's trying to get us to move. To do something, already!

Daimonic energy can feel all-consuming. It's that creative energy that has writers and painters working away long into the night to act on their inspiration, and coax something from the world of imagination into this reality. It's the energy that can overtake us during sex, when we're in a fit of a rage, or the rapture of praise as we listen to a gospel choir.

When we suppress this energy, it can turn into hostility, aggression, cruelty, and violence. The same energy we can use to create can also destroy. That's the link with the word "demon," which is often thought of as an evil force. When we ignore daimonic energy—the energy of our soul—it can take on this "demonic" aspect. Think of how the confinement of prison can create an atmosphere that sometimes feels like a powder keg that could explode at any moment. This is the suppression of daimonic energy. Whether we're channeling the "angels" of our nature or the "demons" has to do with whether we're allowing this vital energy to flow through us, or we're suppressing or ignoring it.

Genius

Daimonic energy is also associated with the concept of genius. Today, we equate genius with a high level of a certain type of intelligence, such as scientific or mathematical ability. Many describe Albert Einstein, Neil deGrasse Tyson, or Steve Jobs as geniuses. Athletes such as LeBron James or Tom Brady also are sometimes praised for athletic genius. We use the word "ingenious" as an adjective to describe something or someone possessing creative or inventive brilliance. But the original meaning of the word is a bit different. Genius wasn't a gift granted only to a few; we all had a genius.

Your archetypes are the form this energy will take. When David Goggins connected with his Warrior archetype, then allowed and even invited daimonic energy to move through him, he became a legend. Again, this was not without a massive amount of hard work and struggle. Goggins had to see what he wanted and grab for it with both hands and wrestle with it over and over. To this day, he continues to grow into even more of himself and continually test his limits. That is part of his Warrior ethos, only at this point he has transformed into the peaceful Warrior, who instead of engaging in any form of outer combat, seeks to master his internal world.

As psychologist Stephen Diamond explains, "Consciousness is the hard-won consequence of insight, and the irreplaceable key to discerning and constructively interacting with the daimonic." Soulmaking is about recognizing the unique set of attributes, skills, and motivations that are deep inside you and learning to live in a way that emphasizes them. Soulmaking is the act of becoming fully aware of our essence, and of engaging our daimon to amplify that essence.

This is how, when a Guard experiences this alignment, you become a Guardian.

"A woman has her Juno, just as a man has his Genius; they are names for the sacred power, the divine spark we each of us have in us. My Juno can't 'get into' me, it is already my deepest self."

~URSULA K. LE GUIN, *LAVINIA*

Integration Exercises

- What did you want to be when you grew up? What about life felt most engaging and interesting? What types of play felt most energizing and rewarding?

- If you enjoy books, movies, or other popular media, what types of stories capture your attention most? What types of characters do you find yourself rooting for, and against?

- When are the times you feel the most *you*? What are you doing? Who are you speaking with? How are you engaging with life?

- What have you noticed is decidedly not you? What creates a feeling of discord or static, discomfort or disease? When does it feel like things are just *off*?

- Where in the world around you do you see your desires and values most reflected? What people or places *resonate* with you, sparking a feeling as if something inside you wakes up and wants to engage with them? If you don't have that experience in the world around you, what about your dreams? If you have recurring dreams that you're flying, for example, is there ever a time in the waking world when you have a similar sense of freedom?

"My mom didn't want me to go into law enforcement. She said once you get behind those gates, you're locked up, too."

~Michelle, who worked in Florida law enforcement as a CO and in other roles for more than 15 years

MAKING SPACE—CLEARING OUT PROJECTIONS AND PAST EXPERIENCES

LESSON 3

Sift through your pain and challenges to find hidden treasures within your experiences. Tap into your true essence and find joy and purpose in your work. Transform your relationship with your career and those you interact with in your life through the power of love and self-awareness.

Being a CO is more than a job; it's a calling. It's one way that the archetype of the Guardian, with its hallmarks of service and empowering others, can play out in someone's life. As you begin to acknowledge the presence of this archetype in your life, to embrace your blueprint, it will start to flourish, and you'll feel enlivened and empowered as you see yourself come alive in your role as a Guardian.

Several times, we've used the analogy of a soul blueprint and of building your home. Now that you're connecting with your blueprint, it's time for the next stage of building, which involves clearing space for construction, including acknowledging and releasing what's been present in your life, especially with regard to your role as a CO, up to this point.

It can be difficult to think that your life and your career could look another way. How are you supposed to imagine this experience of life where COs and those who are incarcerated respect one another and their roles, when just about everything you've experienced up to now has looked nothing like that? How can you believe that another way is possible, especially if you've never seen it?

"As humans, we're reading books every day to try to figure out how to be someone else. What we don't do is go inside, turn ourselves inside out, and read our own story. You have to look inside to find out what you really want."

~DAVID GOGGINS

In the last chapter, we looked at the idea of recognizing your own drives through the lens of someone who wanted to clean out their garage. If you've ever cleaned a garage, a closet, or anywhere else there's accumulated mess, you know the first step is taking everything off the shelves and sifting through it so you can determine what you want to keep and what you want to get rid of. This makes the mess appear even bigger. You're standing there, up to your knees in all the junk you've accumulated, thinking, *"This looks even worse! Maybe I should have just left all of this stuff where it was."* But once everything's unpacked and out there in front of you, you notice something miraculous. The shelves are completely clean! You've got a clean slate. Now you can begin to imagine something different. First, you've got to go through that messy but necessary ritual of clearing the shelves.

The Challenge of Confinement

The first stage of clearing is acknowledging what's already there. In your case, it's taking a noncritical but honest look at everything you've experienced up to now.

Previously, we discussed the idea that COs and incarcerated individuals have much in common, largely due to the circumstances they share. After all, day after day, year after year, you're confined to a similar space. Sure, you get days off here and there, but most of your time, you experience the pressure and stress of confinement, even when you're not working. Chances are your work has a serious impact on your psyche—on how you experience life and how you relate to others.

"We joke in Corrections that we hate people. It's not that. It's just we've seen the worst, so it's difficult to have trust and want to be in crowds and be available to people emotionally. I've seen some of the physical aspects of myself, weight gain, weight loss, fatigue, and things others have gone through because this industry is very taxing on us."

~GREG, A CO WHO HAS SERVED AS A MASTER KEY CONTROL SERGEANT, MEMBER OF A SPECIAL OPERATIONS RESPONSE TEAM, CORRECTIONS COUNSELOR, AMONG OTHER ROLES

CO Michelle struggled for years with the pressures of her surroundings. "I was so upset, I was ready to walk off and leave these inmates by themselves. I really did need the job for my family, though, so I had to toughen up and get to a point where I could just go in and detach from my emotions enough to do the job. Doing that made me kind of mean and hardened my heart. I started treating the inmates poorly. I have to say, I did not like my job for the first ten years." At one point, Michelle had a seizure that doctors told her was likely due to stress.

You know your job is challenging, and yet you've probably created some kind of structure to help yourself deal with it day to day. Maybe that structure involves numbing and shutting down, maybe it involves acting out (in ways healthy or unhealthy), maybe something else, or a combination. Even if you've developed some coping mechanisms or an operating structure that isn't especially healthy, it's gotten you to this point, and so in some ways it has worked. There's no need to feel you've done something wrong or to spend time being hard on yourself; as humans, in every moment, we're all using the resources we have at hand to devise solutions to challenges. No less, no more. Given more resources, we have more options. This work is about expanding your awareness of the resources in life that are available to you, which are broader and richer than you've been aware of to this point.

Embracing What Is

Before we continue, there's a point that must be acknowledged. Speaking of the future and of what might be is in some ways a dangerous game. When we become too focused on an imagined future, we forego the satisfaction and even the joy of being in our lives exactly as they are right now. When we speak of the Guardian archetype and what's possible, keep in mind we're talking about a new way of being that's enabled by recognizing what is true *right now*, at this very minute.

These skills, this nobility, this honor, this heart, this strength, this compassion *are already inside you*. What we're working on now is clearing out obstacles to the full realization of who you are. In many ways, throughout this process, life on the outside won't appear different. The prison system, your direct supervisor, or anyone else, won't change overnight because of this shift. What *will* change is how you relate to all of it. In that way, what is true in this future we speak of is already true now, waiting to be recognized and engaged with in a new way.

When you acknowledge all of the painful experiences and ways of relating to your work you have known to this point, it's also not about judging those things as bad or wrong or saying they shouldn't have happened. Instead, it's about observing them all so that you can relate openly and honestly with what is. No more stuffing things away in boxes. No more hiding your "junk" from family and friends.

Think again about the idea of victim consciousness. It's easy to perceive yourself to be a victim of all that's happened. Here, you are choosing another way to look at what you've experienced. Imagine that when you were born, someone placed over your eyes a pair of glasses where the lenses allowed only a very small view of the world. You could only see what was directly in front of you, and then, only a tiny bit of it. This happened at such a young age you aren't even aware that you're wearing these glasses. Then, one day, you're out for a walk and come upon a lake. As you bend down to look into the lake, the water is so clear and pure that for the first time, you see your true reflection, glasses and all. Confused, you reach up toward your eyes and touch the glasses, then remove them. At first, you may be overwhelmed with your new, expanded vision, and feel an urge to put the glasses back on, but slowly, as you look around, you take in the beauty that's all around you, you realize this beauty was there all along, it was just that your view was obscured. When we choose to remove our victim glasses, we become open to the full, lush beauty of the vast resources both inside and around us. Again, it can be an adjustment to take all this in, and to accept the responsibility and accountability for how powerful we truly are, but in doing so, we open up worlds of possibility that before were invisible to us.

As Armor Down founder Ben King noted, when we open to the ability to be with all that is, we access more thoughtful and effective tools for dealing with situations, along with the clear sight to know when and how to use them. We cannot do this from a consciousness that is entirely self-absorbed. Nor can we do this from a consciousness that is not at all concerned with our self. If you tend to focus entirely on others and their needs and

"I say, follow your bliss and don't be afraid, and doors will open where you didn't know they were going to be. If you follow your bliss, doors will open for you that wouldn't have opened for anyone else."

~JOSEPH CAMPBELL

experiences, again, you lose the full picture. When we focus on noticing all that is, that includes our own thoughts, feelings, and motivations.

This work is not meant to disconnect you from your pain, but rather to help you understand and embrace it so you can make use of the gifts and guidance it offers. You have felt pain around your work because you care. Because you love. That is beautiful and worthwhile. And it's that love that we want to hold onto and amplify. Your pain is one of your greatest guides, because it represents your purpose. When we learn to integrate our pain into our lives, we can then show others how to do the same. Joseph Campbell referred to taking on our own pain as part of the hero's journey. Instead of "slaying the dragon" of our pain, we're meant to befriend it. In so doing, we swallow our pain—not suppressing it, but ingesting and metabolizing it. In this way, by fully coming to understand it and developing a relationship with it, it becomes something that fuels and directs us. Campbell wrote, "The demon that you can swallow gives you its power, and the greater life's pain, the greater life's reply."

Through this process of remembering your true self, you won't stop feeling pain. In fact in some ways and at some times, your pain will be magnified. Seeing the anger, despair, and fear all around you will continue to hurt because you will continue to love, and to love even more. The pain will not disappear, but you will relate to it differently, as part of your purpose and as something that empowers you as a Guardian.

If you've found ways to dull or numb the pain you've felt, it's time to reconnect with these uncomfortable feelings. Remember that when you suppress what you feel, no matter what those feelings are, you suppress life. And that daimonic energy will start to take the demonic form, affecting your health and your wellbeing, and causing you to act out of alignment with your essence.

Through this work, what will change is how you relate to the suffering that you see every day. Instead of becoming angry or feeling the need to shut down and numb, or to act out, you will engage with all you experience from your Guardian self.

Part of this process is learning how to see your pain as your power—as the source of the substance that will not only fuel your work in this world, but help you feel a sense of place and belonging here, as well as purpose. An early step in seeing pain this way is learning to sift through your pain for the treasures that lie there.

Sifting Through Pain

When you stand before your building site and see everything that lies before you—all of your prior experiences, you don't just go in with a bulldozer and push it all aside. If you don't first sift through what's there, what you rebuild is destined to look a whole lot like what was there before.

You can think of this process like an archeological dig. When an archeologist goes to a site and begins to sift through the dirt and debris, plenty of it will simply be accumulated junk that's not worth keeping. Yet there will also be treasures deeply hidden. One of the ways archeologists determine where they're likely to find these treasures is by locating clues, such as evidence of old structures. Within our own hearts and minds, pain is one of our clues to buried treasure.

"Pain is the biggest power of love."
~STEPHEN KING

Everything we experience in life, whether we deem it positive or negative, carries the potential for learning. Until we acquire this intended knowledge, we'll continue to experience these learning opportunities over and over. In prison, for example, you're presented again and again with opportunities to learn how your words and actions impact others within this specialized environment of confinement, interacting with people from whom love has mostly, or entirely, been withheld. Until you open to seeing these opportunities for what they are and receiving their lessons, you are likely to experience them similarly, over and over.

Pain—and the fear, anxiety, disgust, and so on that it presents as—is like a flashing neon sign that shouts, "Lesson!" But pain isn't just associated with negative feelings.

The first time you held your newborn child, when a parent said, "I'm proud of you," when a spouse said, "I love you," or when a prison resident said, "Thank you for treating me with dignity," these experiences, too, can feel painful. It's the piercing sensation of exquisite beauty. It's like when you've been out in the cold for a long time and your fingers and toes have numbed, then you step in front of the glow of a warm fire and the blood rushes in. It hurts. So much so that you might have to fight the urge to move away from these experiences instead of fully taking them in. The challenge is in staying with painful experiences, whether positive or negative, to receive what they have to offer.

We believe that God, in any way we understand God, intends for us to experience joy and freedom. It would hold, then, that we have within us the ability to be joyous and free anywhere. When CO Michelle recognized this ability within herself, her entire relationship with her work, which she had experienced as extremely stressful, shifted. She changed how she related to the work. She saw negative situations not as those to shut down and run from, but as those where love was needed. She stopped resisting the joy and freedom that have the potential to be recognized in every moment.

There's a saying we embrace, which is that the poison is often the medicine. What can seem like a wound can also be the source of tremendous growth and personal power. The Japanese have a special art called *kintsugi*, which translates to "golden joinery." It involves taking pottery that's been cracked or broken and repairing it with a lacquer that's dusted or mixed with powdered gold, silver, or platinum. Precious materials applied to the cracks in this way do not hide, but emphasize them, and indeed create an entirely new piece of art. By employing *kintsugi*, the artist emphasizes that the break is not a mistake or in any way unfortunate, but rather is simply part of the history of the piece, which has now become something new. In this way, cracks, though unintentional, are celebrated and appreciated. We can learn to view and work with the cracks in our lives similarly, applying gold to our broken places instead of attempting to hide them.

For Michelle, the fear and anxiety she experienced showed her where she was engaging in victim consciousness, and when she accepted that realization, she was able to shift her perspective. From that point on, the way she experienced her role as CO changed. Her circumstances stayed the same, but now life energy flowed through her freely and she connected with her essence and her passion to serve others. She began to experience *eudaimonia*.

When you're standing there and someone is yelling in your face, it's absurd to imagine feeling joyful. But is it? If you can pan out and switch to that moviegoer mode, observing what's happening, seeing there is pain present that this person is expressing, you can also see that this is an indication that the soul is at work. That the soul is wanting to engage with *daimonic* energy—the energy of life—but the atmosphere of confinement has restricted its expression, so it's coming out in its *demonic* form. The question, then, becomes: How can you create more freedom in this situation? How can you provide a setting in which this person feels they can express that energy constructively? Often, through an act so outwardly simple as listening with no agenda other than to truly hear, we can open a massive amount of space for the fruitful flow of energy.

This is how we learn to sift through pain to see the opportunities for soul-centered action and interaction that nurtures. In the same way we identify these treasures for others, we must learn to identify them for ourselves. And so now we are back to acknowledging our pain.

Our pain is. That is all. It does not define you, but it does indicate some critical things about you, including where you are challenged to give or to receive love.

Going forward, you can begin to perceive pain this way, and when you encounter it in yourself or others, ask, *What is painful about this moment? What is the role of love in this moment? Where is love needed that I can provide it?* Think of the incarcerated individual who is struggling to deal with the fact that he is missing his daughter's fifth birthday. Or, *Where is love being offered that I am struggling to receive it?* Think of your own daughter wanting to connect with you after your shift by telling you about her day at school.

"Pain insists upon being attended to. God whispers to us in our pleasures, speaks in our consciences, but shouts in our pains. It is His megaphone to rouse a deaf world."

~C.S. LEWIS

Notice how, either way, your connection to love both deepens and broadens when you can be present with pain. In addition to being present with pain, another way to clear the debris is to open to the possibilities for greater freedom that exist within confinement.

Reimagining Confinement

CO Brian said, "Family and friends will tell me I'm not the same person I was when I started the job. I could see the change now when I leave the store. If I go into a restaurant, once I sit down and look around, I realize I have positioned myself so nothing can come behind me. You don't trust people like you used to. You start to believe everybody's trying to con you, inmates and management. We don't talk to our families about what we see and what we have to do on some days. It's devastating."

Look at the building site before you and take in this devastation as it appears in your own life. Take it in. But remember, too, that within that devastation lies treasure.

Just as restriction and confinement can be devastating, they can also be enriching. When we embrace what is, we find that life presents us with unending paradox, where multiple things that seem contradictory can all be true. When we judge a situation, we take a side, choosing only one possibility and cutting off the other. Confinement is devastating. If we forego judgment and take that wider view, all that confinement can be devastating, and it can also be enriching. Both things can be true. And so our choice becomes evident. Which experience will you have? Which will you seek to enable for others?

Just like the confined space and shape of a cup enables us to receive water from a faucet or a river so we can drink it, any kind of structure that creates a boundary or constricts what's available to us can actually be helpful. We can see this limitation as a tool or an opportunity. In fact, social psychologists say that one of the reasons so many people are unhappy these days is that we experience far too much choice. We're overwhelmed by possibilities. While possibility is a wonderful thing, if we're attuned more to what's outside us than what's inside us, it can confound our efforts to connect with our own true essence. Instead, we focus on what we *should* do, want, or choose according to others' ideas and opinions.

Science also shows that, ironically, when we have fewer options, we tend to be happier with what we do choose. And we also tend to be more creative with what we make. Think of the game Scrabble. If we simply had access to unlimited letter tiles and could make any words we wanted, there would be no challenge, and so there would be no fun. Instead, the restriction of having access to only a certain selection of letters, along with whatever words are currently on the board that you can build from, forces you to become more engaged and creative, and the result is that when you create something that works, it's exciting, joyful, and satisfying.

You can think of your blueprint the same way. In some ways, it limits what you can do in your life to experience eudaimonia because you must act in accordance with your own unique plan. Yet at the same time, within that plan, there are endless ways to embody and express the essence of who you are.

Acknowledging What Is

Most likely, you haven't been given the tools or training necessary to make your work as a CO a eudaemonic experience. For example, as Brian expressed in Lesson 2, being seen as someone in charge of warehousing the incarcerated rather than playing an active role in the quality and outcomes of people's experience is frustrating and even painful. This lack of provision of resources that would help you experience your work as a Guardian is part of the debris spread out before you, and perhaps is a source of pain and frustration for you, as well.

Let's acknowledge that. Again, you don't need to do so with judgment or blame. This is simply about looking at it and saying, "I see you." To this point, it's likely that just about everything related to your work has been framed as a potential problem rather than an opportunity for learning and growth for both you and those in your care. If that angers or irritates you, that's a good thing. It means you care. It means you are deeply connected to your work. As psychologist Rollo May explains, the opposite of love is not hatred, but apathy. Apathy indicates a disengagement. Where there is irritation, frustration, even rage, there is passion. There is life energy. And like clay on a potter's wheel, we can shape that energy by deciding how we wish to engage with and express it.

At this point you may be wondering, *How can I make a difference? If I am only one, operating inside a system, how can I change my experience?* When the road ahead is obscured by such problem-centered thinking, it's easy to feel a sense of ineffectiveness or paralysis about your situation. You see that what you're directed to do in some cases, perhaps many, is not only ineffective, in some respects it's nonsensical. There is not rehabilitation, there is storage. Instead of being given the opportunity to work together with those who are incarcerated to support their experience so that it may have some benefit for them, you are in many cases tasked and given resources only to ensure that they behave according to the rules, and to subdue them should they become *unruly* and push back. We may even perceive this arrangement to be noble—that the CO is following orders and carrying out their duty in an honorable way. And yet what you see and experience in the day-to-day does not support this perception. Deep inside you know this is not the way. That things can be done more effectively when you engage your compassion and your humanity. Your essence tells you that the way you're being directed to do your job is not the noble way.

In *Iron John: A Book About Men*, author and poet Robert Bly describes how in our modern industrial era, men, especially (though this idea applies across gender), have been told it is their role to subdue nature. The belief is that nature is somehow disruptive and dangerous, that humans are separate from nature, and the role of protectors is to dominate and control nature for the good of society. If we believe our ability to access the noble states of love, freedom, power, and connection are contingent on carrying this out, we will do it at any cost. This becomes a source of pain because some part of us knows these actions are out of alignment not only with the nature outside us, but with our own internal nature, and that in fact the two are deeply linked. We know domination of a human being's nature, too, is not the way.

In many cases, those who are incarcerated are viewed somehow as some lesser form of human, as part of wild savage nature, to be controlled and subdued. If you as a CO are put in the position of enforcing this ethos, through your actions to subdue wild nature you become distanced from you own connection with nature. Separation from nature is the definition of human suffering. We cannot be separated from the nature outside of us without also being separated from the nature within us. We cannot seek to separate others from nature without causing pain for ourselves. It is completely understandable that, put in this untenable position, you would become angry or depressed, and turn to anything that would help dull the pain of this disconnect.

Yet in spite of this common directive to subdue nature, many COs seek another way. Gary, who served as a CO for nearly three decades, recognized the importance of preserving the humanity of those he worked with. "I was really good with interpersonal communications and treated the prisoners as people no matter the crime. I presented tasks in a way that allowed them to feel human. I wasn't just another RoboCop barking orders. A lot of people think that if you say 'Thank you' to an inmate you have belittled yourself. Well, if the inmate just cleaned up the whole dorm, I was going to say thank you for doing a good job. They appreciated that acknowledgment of their humanity." In this way, Gary, like so many COs, sought another way to carry out his duty. Rather than trying to dominate, subdue, and control, he provided recognition and support. He provided love.

This mirrors an approach practiced by some healthcare practitioners. In Western medicine, the more common approach to healthcare is to focus on disease control. A disease or disorder

"We do not see nature with our eyes, but with our understandings and our hearts."

~WILLIAM HAZLITT

is identified and attacked, usually using medications or surgeries. Other practitioners, especially in Eastern modalities, take a different approach. Instead of focusing exclusively on the disease or disorder, the practitioner looks for the health. They identify what in the body is working, but needs more resources to be successful. For example, they may focus on supporting the immune system by prescribing healthful foods, drinks, or herbs, increased sleep, or anything else that can remove the barriers and challenges preventing the immune system doing its job effectively. In his way, Gary was identifying and supporting the health.

When we support the health, we ask, *What's working here? What's positive that we want to encourage?* You can also ask these questions when you look within yourself.

Instead of focusing on dominating or eradicating the disease, health practitioners center their attention on the inherent intelligence already at work. They recognize that there is an organizing structure and a natural order at work that they can *let go into*. Specifically, the body's constant drive and ability to heal itself. Instead of trying to force a change, they provide loving and attentive support to the natural healing mechanisms already at work. They participate in healing. They cocreate it. And to do so they employ responsiveness more than dominance.

As psychologist Bill Plotkin writes, "We foster wholeness in ourselves when we contribute to the wholeness of something greater than ourselves. ... When we're centered in the consciousness of our Nurturing Adult, we're able to accept everything about other people. We understand—or attempt to understand—each characteristic, trait, or state of others as a coherent feature of those individuals, part of what makes them who they are. Naturally, some human traits—such as violence, hatred, or greed—are deeply troubling, but we sense how such characteristics are expressions of others' current conditions." Again, this is reminiscent of how CO Gary describes the way he interacted with those in his care.

When asked why it's common for people driving past prisons to look away, a sheriff at the Mendocino County Jail replied, "I think the shame people feel when they look away is that in their guts they know that there is a process of human rehabilitation that is supposed to be happening in prison and it is not."

Part of it may also be that prisons house the unrecognized shadow of our collective society. Sarah Kerr, a ritual healing practitioner who specializes in death and grief, says many ancient societies have a tradition of scapegoating—of pushing people to the margins on whom they project their own shadow so they don't have to confront what is inside them. Someone who has committed a transgression, real or perceived, is cast out and then we turn away from them. We don't want to look too closely at someone we think of as a criminal because they may look more familiar to us than we care to acknowledge. It is this lack of identification with our own shadow qualities—the recognition that under certain circumstances we, too, could find ourselves behind prison walls—that keeps us from having compassion for others.

Many COs, being up close and personal with these scapegoats, know different. As Bill Plotkin says, they can sense the conditions that have contributed to the present circumstances of those in prison. Because of this, COs hold some of the greatest potential in our culture for change. Kyle, a former CO in Arizona, said, "Sometimes I would see these inmates and wonder what they must have experienced to get to this place. Sometimes it just broke my heart to see these people who had no support system at all, nobody to reach out to. And now they're probably in the worst place they could possibly be. Don't get me wrong—I knew they were inmates. But I'm not a judge, and at a certain point I had to stop thinking about what they were in there for."

Keith Hellwig, who worked as a CO for 36 years, said, "As a Correctional Officer, you're dealing with people whose existence the general public doesn't even want to acknowledge. I've dealt with many serial killers and serial rapists, but as a Correctional Officer you can't think of them as just a killer or a rapist. That isn't their whole identity, and you have to think of them as complete individuals. I remember escorting Jeffrey Dahmer to a facility and still feeling a strong sense of duty to protect him. You have to treat these felons as people. Throughout my career, I've tried to treat everyone the way I would want to be treated if I were incarcerated. I considered them humans above everything else—because that's what they are. These prisoners, no matter what they've done, still have people who love them. They're still somebody's son, daughter, somebody's nephew, or somebody's father or mother."

As we've observed in our own work, the people who society marginalizes carry within them the most unlocked potential, and it is their treasures society needs the most. Indeed, it is *your* treasures society needs the most, because just as we marginalize prison residents, you, too, are marginalized by association. We need your gifts.

We believe that when you change the relationship COs have with those in prison, you change the relationship people in prison have with the world. When you change the relationship people in prison have with the world, you change the relationship prisons have with the world. Journalist and author Sydney J. Harris wrote, "Most people are mirrors, reflecting the moods and emotions of the times; few are windows, bringing light to bear on the dark corners where troubles fester. The whole purpose of education is to turn mirrors into windows." Your task is similar.

For guards to function as Guardians—to become the priests in the monastery—it is incumbent upon you to attend to your own awakening with integrity. That is no small responsibility, and no small undertaking. That is the path of the Leader.

Recognizing the Consequences

Acknowledging what is includes recognizing that everything has consequences. They are a natural outcome of our interactions with others. We often use phrases such as, "You'll have to deal with the consequences," implying that consequences are negative. In reality, they are neutral—they are simply a result. The consequence of Oshea Israel's killing of Laramiun Byrd was a prison sentence. Another consequence was a long-term, loving

"If you plan on being anything less than you are capable of being, you will probably be unhappy all the days of your life."

~ABRAHAM MASLOW

relationship with Laramiun's mother, Mary Johnson. This was not an outcome Oshea Israel could have scripted, controlled, or predicted. We can easily look at Oshea Israel's choice to pull that trigger as wrong or bad, and yet he and Mary Johnson have gone on to inspire love and forgiveness in countless others.

When we acknowledge that, again, the web in which all of our lives is woven is vast beyond our perception, we begin to release judgments of good and bad. There are actions and consequences, and there is a math to it all beyond our immediate understanding.

Your own actions are a tapping on that web, sending vibrations out into directions you cannot see. Some of the consequences of your actions will be relatively predictable, but many will not be, and you will never witness or be aware of these consequences.

As you move forward in this work, know that the most and the best any of us can do is to be in congruence within ourselves. To remember our essence. To allow life energy to animate us as we embody our blueprint. If we do these things, we can release the rest to the greater structure, one far more vast that we can comprehend, that is at work. We can trust that the consequences of our actions will fit the grand equation in whatever way they're intended.

Integration Exercises

- When you "empty your shelves" and look into the piles surrounding you, what is there that is valuable and that you want to keep? To nurture? To build on?

"Healing is a different type of pain. It's the pain of becoming aware of the power of one's strength and weakness, of one's capacity to love or do damage to oneself and to others, and of how the most challenging person to control in life is ultimately yourself."

~CAROLINE MYSS

- What are you ready to discard?

- When you sift through the stuff, where do you come upon pain? What is the potential treasure in this pain? In what ways is love speaking to you through this pain?

- What "poison" have you had to ingest? How can you imagine that this poison could also be some of your greatest medicine?

- What health do you see around you? What is working that you can support? What about within you?

"Corrections Officers need help and support because they're dying on the inside, but they won't ask anybody for help."

~Greg, a CO who has served as a Master Key Control Sergeant, member of a Special Operations Response Team, Corrections Counselor, among other roles

THE TOLL OF TRAUMA

LESSON 4

Discover how trauma can be a powerful tool for personal growth and resilience. Learn to use your pain as a catalyst for creating a fulfilling and flourishing life as you anchor yourself in the vision of what is possible.

COs and incarcerated individuals are inextricably and powerfully linked in a dance of your own becoming. There's an old saying that when the student is ready, the teacher will appear. In many ways, that teacher cannot become a teacher until someone assumes the mantle of the student, and the student can't fully embody that role until someone steps forward and embraces the identity of teacher. We might say that when the prison resident is ready to accept the mantle of monk, the Guardian will appear, and when the guard is ready to step into their wholeness as a Guard, the prison resident will blossom into the monk.

Yet as we've acknowledged, the path is neither easy nor clear. That is purposeful, because it is the journey that shapes us. Recall our discussion of the hero's journey in Lesson 2. The purpose of the journey is not to reach a final destination, but to experience the journey and grow in the process. To interact with seemingly insurmountable challenges and in so doing connect with our deepest selves, including the drives, motivations, and skills that are hidden within us and long to be recognized and engaged.

Along this journey, one of the skillsets we're invited to develop is the ability to interact with pain and trauma in a *generative* way. Classically, we are taught that pain, suffering, agony—all of these things are bad and should be avoided at all costs, yet if you wish to experience a life in a way worth living, a life alive with connection, engagement, and meaning, this isn't possible. Instead of spending our precious energy trying to suppress trauma, we can learn to engage with it in a way that it can serve us.

How Trauma Can Serve Us

Once, there was a young prince who was beloved by his parents. They loved him so much that they decided they would do everything they could to shelter him from the suffering of the world, and so they kept him confined to the palace grounds. The boy grew into a man, he married a beautiful, loving woman, and fathered a child. Yet the man who would one day be King couldn't escape the persistent feeling that he was missing out on something. He couldn't explain it, but in spite of all he had, he felt a sense of emptiness inside. So, one day, he decided to set forth from the palace and explore the countryside, and he was shocked by what he saw. People suffering from hunger, from illness, perpetrating crimes against one another... He was both heartbroken and baffled by all of this pain. What could be the purpose of all this suffering? He searched for the greatest teachers he could find, he fasted and endured other austerities, all in search of the meaning of life. Still, it eluded him. So, he decided he would try something different—he would sit down under a tree and meditate until the answer revealed itself to him. For 49 days he sat under the tree, and while he sat, he was assaulted by insecurity, anxiety, fear, and desire, yet he stayed where he was, still and at peace. Finally, he experienced a sensation he'd never felt before, a sense of connectedness with absolutely everything in the world. Every being, every plant, every beam of light and dark shadow—he was one with them all. When the man opened his eyes, he was transformed. The prince, once named Siddhartha, had become the Buddha, a name that means "he who is awake."

What awareness or knowledge did the Buddha awaken to? Did he discover a way to numb or subvert pain so he would never have to experience suffering? In fact, no, he discovered the opposite. The Buddha discovered that it is our *resistance to pain*, and not the pain itself, that causes suffering. When we can be present with all that is in life, including pain, instead of trying to suppress or run from it, we alleviate suffering. Instead, how we typically experience pain is to react as if it is wrong; that pain shouldn't exist; that it's not *fair* that we should experience pain. What the Buddha realized is that pain is as joy is. Each is essential to a life fully lived, and to deny or rage against pain is to limit joy, and to resist life itself.

How Trauma Builds Resilience

You've likely heard the saying, "That which doesn't kill me only makes me stronger." This can be true, yet unfortunately most of us never learn *how* to transform our trauma into resilience. Left to our own devices, we think if we merely survive, we'll somehow thrive, so we try to just get through it. We try to endure our pain and stuff it down, believing the victory is simply waking up again the next day. All the while, we become more and more distant and disconnected from our true essence.

Perhaps you have been told by others, overtly or passively, that the way to deal with trauma is to not deal with it. Maybe you saw this in your family growing up—that one or another of your parents would deal with pain, sorrow, or grief by trying to suppress or ignore it. Perhaps a supervisor told you to shut yourself off to what you'd be seeing inside prison walls. To somehow try to not be affected by it; that vulnerability is weakness, and guards can never be weak. "They teach us to leave it at the gate," says former CO Michael. The result, as warden Charles describes it, is that, "You almost become non-human, robotic, emotionless."

As clinical psychologist Daniel Kriegman describes, when we deal with pain and trauma by suppressing it, it's like creating a clogged pipe. Instead, we need to learn to interact with our pain in ways that let it keep moving, or it will block the flow of everything. There was an old commercial for Draino that showed the inside of a pipe where a clog was lodged. When water was poured into the pipe, it stopped at the clog. Nothing could get past it. When we suppress our emotions, we create this kind of blockage inside ourselves, and nothing can get past it. Not even joy. We begin to feel cut off from our ability to feel much of anything at all. And this not only cuts us off from ourselves, it isolates us from others, as well.

> *"Officers can never be weak. Inmates can never be weak. It's its own world."*
>
> ~BRIAN, HEAD OF A MEDICAL EVALUATION UNIT

As humans, as we described earlier, our brains are designed for connection. We long to experience *limbic resonance*, in which we can sync up with others, feel seen and acknowledged by them, experience empathy, and so on. When we have these blockages in our system, that blockage caused by trauma and pain becomes our focus. As we fixate on our suffering, we turn away from others, and that lack of connection and the experience of resonance with others causes more suffering. It causes a deep hunger inside us that we don't know how to feed. When we feel it, because we don't know what it is or how to deal with it healthfully, we try to numb it through substances, television, social media, video games, food...anything that offers some semblance of comfort. Yet these things leave us craving more, because they don't resolve the true source of our deep hunger—our need for connection.

Then, eventually, something snaps. The pressure against the blockage is too strong, and we break down. We may consider taking our own lives, we may overdose, we may fly into a violent rage. These are all manifestations of the daimonic or life-force energy inside of us yearning to move, trying to create a force strong enough to flush out that blockage. When daimonic energy is suppressed, it can be expressed in outbursts. This is neither good nor bad, it simply is. It is life-force energy longing to move through us freely once again.

Perhaps you've experienced this in a lesser way. Maybe you had a rough day when a prison resident was getting under your skin, when you felt irritated with your partner, when a friend said something that made you angry and you did something to "blow off steam." You went out and played basketball, hit the gym, blasted music in your car, went out dancing, or took part in some other activity that allowed you to move your energy. This is a healthy way of dealing with trauma, because what you did was allow that daimonic energy to flow through you rather than fester.

After working as a CO, Michelle went on to work in the communications department for a sheriff's office. "I received a call about a young man who killed himself. His friend found him, then his mom showed up on the scene. You have to stay on the phone until a deputy gets there, and there's a professional protocol you must follow. I'm on the phone, listening to the screaming, the crying, to the mother that just found her child. I would listen with tears rolling down my face. Then when I hung up, I would go outside and cry or scream because it's hard not to be compassionate. It's hard not to be human." Even though she had to follow a protocol while she was on the phone, as soon as she had a chance, instinctively Michelle allowed herself to let that energy of trauma, of empathy, and of humanity flow through her. She literally gave voice to her pain.

As Daniel Kriegman explains, we are actually designed not only to deal with traumatic events, but to use these events to become stronger and more resilient. Years ago, scientists in Arizona created an experiment where they constructed a "biodome" that housed everything necessary to sustain life, then lived inside it for two years and studied the patterns of nature inside it. There were a few problems, though, including the fact that for some reason, the trees had trouble growing. It befuddled the scientists. There was nutritious soil, ample light... Then, they realized what was missing—wind. The "perfect" environment had no wind, and without the pressure created by wind, prompting the trees to strengthen to withstand it, they didn't become strong enough to thrive even in a windless environment. Their core— their heartwood—was too weak for them to thrive. Trauma and pain are the wind that strengthens our heartwood.

Richard Tedeschi, a psychologist and researcher at UNC Charlotte, was looking for his next project. "Who do I want to know more about?" he asked himself. His answer: People who are wise. His question: How did they get that way? He realized he'd seen a lot of wisdom among people who'd endured great challenges, so he and fellow UNC psychologist-researcher Lawrence Calhoun undertook a project where they interviewed 600 people who'd experienced serious trauma—they'd lost a spouse or survived a severe injury that left them paralyzed, for instance. In their research, a pattern emerged. Over and over

"Pain nourishes courage. You can't be brave if you've only had wonderful things happen to you."

~MARY TYLER MOORE

again, the interviewees said that while they wished the experience hadn't happened, in some ways it had changed them for the better. The team isolated five key areas where people noted improvements: they appreciated life more, they were aware of more possibilities in life, their relationships were better, they felt more spiritual fulfillment, and overall, they felt stronger. As a result of their research, Tedeschi and Calhoun coined the term "post-traumatic growth" to describe how people can actually become stronger as a result of trauma. According to their research, as many as 90 percent of people who've experienced serious trauma say that at least one aspect of their life is better as a result of their experience. In a study of Vietnam War veterans who'd been captured, 61 percent said they'd benefitted in some way from the experience.

Every superhero has an origin story—some series of experiences that were challenging or even devastating, but that helped them to connect with the deep reservoir of strength inside them. To overcome those experiences required them to call on every resource inside them, and once those resources were engaged, they were forever changed into the fullest, richest version of themselves.

Daniel Kriegman says, "Traumatic experience is intertwined with our mortal lives. In a life fully lived, agony is inevitable. Yet chronic suffering is not at all inevitable. … We are designed to face the painful aspects of our existence and find some way to rise above them. Indeed, once activated, post-traumatic growth can be used in the service of creating a life centered in eudaimonia."

"A good half of the art of living is resilience."

~ALAIN DE BOTTON

As life begins to flow within us, we can start to feel the emotions that have been trapped. And when we begin to release trauma, one of the most common feelings we experience is grief.

Making Space for Grief

It's likely that to this point, among the emotions both you and those in your care have been suppressing is grief. As you begin to acknowledge and release trauma, it's very likely that feelings of grief and mourning for what has been will arise. This is natural and normal, though it may not feel natural and normal for you if you've been told over and over you have to "be strong." As we reframe what strength really is, remember that we become stronger when we stay with what is—when we refrain from trying to suppress or run from it. Like the tree standing strong, you can experience grief as something as normal and natural as the wind, and as a force that when we're present with it, strengthens us.

As much as possible, allow any grief that arises through this acknowledgment of trauma to flow through you. If you're in the habit of suppressing it, it may feel foreign and uncomfortable to let your grief move through you. When we've starved or suppressed our emotions for some time, when we begin to feel again, when we begin to thaw, it can be painful. It's like the blood rushing back into frostbitten fingers and limbs—it can hurt at first to experience this warmth of feeling returning and rushing through you. But this blood and this warmth are restoring your vitality and your aliveness.

Going through this experience of being present with and allowing your own grief not only helps this energy move through you but will help you recognize when those in your care are experiencing grief, as well. Walking this path, first, prepares you to support them as their own grief arises. You'll also be better equipped to be a present and supportive spouse, parent, and friend.

Another aspect of grief that you may feel rising up within you is over the loss of what seems like it has been taken from you: the ability to show love and compassion and to be vulnerable and to express your true self. As CO Andy described it, "The one thing that's stolen most from Corrections Officers is their ability to be vulnerable. You can't really experience love unless you allow yourself to be completely vulnerable to it and what comes with it—the hurt, the joy, and everything that can be part of a much more amazing experience. It's a travesty really."

This concept of loss is a source of pain that must be acknowledged, as well. Yet as you acknowledge it, remember that

"Out of suffering have emerged the strongest souls; the most massive characters are seared with scars."

~KHALIL GIBRAN

your true heart, your essence, has *not* actually been taken from you. It has been hidden. Covered up. The fact that this is a source of pain and grief actually demonstrates and underscores that you are still connected to your care and your compassion. That you have *not* lost the ability for love and connection. That is the treasure in the pain—the discovery that your drive to show love is so strong that it has persisted in spite of all the obstacles you've experienced to this point.

In this process, you can acknowledge the pain of the perception that your essence was lost. That you may have felt beyond the reach of loved ones and even yourself. At the same time, you can allow yourself to experience joy over the dawning awareness that who you are can never actually be taken from you. You were there all along, and your essence remains untouched by the trauma within and around you.

The Trauma of Shared Suffering

You have experienced trauma, and so, too, have those in your care. In fact, much of your relationship to this point has likely been a union based largely in shared suffering. As you make the choice to move beyond the realm of suffering and victimhood into an experience of life in which you understand and embrace your own tremendous capacity to shape all of your experiences, it's necessary to fully acknowledge what has been.

Think of it as a type of closure. It's not that you are meant to forget what you and those you care for have experienced. Instead, you are choosing to release the trauma of *how* you've been experiencing past events to the history. You are burying it in the soil not to hide it, but so it can become part of the rich loam and fertilizer that will nourish your future. When we acknowledge trauma and heartfully release it, we *welcome* all that has been, including and especially that which has caused us pain, because it has brought us to where we are, and it will help to inform where we are going. We are not grateful for the pain, but for the knowledge and awareness we can extract from it.

"Grief does not change you... It reveals you."

~JOHN GREEN

"Pain makes me grow. Growing is what I want. Therefore, for me, pain is pleasure."

~ARNOLD SCHWARZENEGGER

Acknowledging Trauma Among Incarcerated Individuals

We're not going to try to tell you what you already know—after all, who knows better than you what prison residents experience on a day-to-day basis? This section isn't meant to tell you anything new, rather we seek to be present with you in acknowledging the horrors that many, perhaps most, who experience incarceration endure. In this way, we are sharing with you the burden of this awareness, as you have had to carry it by yourself for far too long. Indeed, the responsibility of what those who are incarcerated experience belongs to all of society, and we wish to honor and accept our part and our role in that.

Incarceration takes from individuals the status of productive members of society. Because of this, incarcerated individuals can experience a loss of a sense of purpose in life. As you've no doubt seen, incarcerated individuals can feel a loss of identity and sense of self. Their skills, talents, intelligence, go unacknowledged, causing a further sense of separation from their essence and their soul. There is also the trauma of separation from their families— missing out on milestones such as birthdays, graduations, funerals, and other observances, and being unable to help them in times of need. On top of it, there is the ongoing stress of physical confinement and the fear of violence.

We acknowledge that the act of withholding love, compassion, and connection from anyone suppresses that which wants to come alive within each of us. That it creates active blocks to one's ability to connect with and express their soul. In this way, we as a society have created and enabled environments that willfully suppress those living in prisons' abilities to experience life in any way other than what they have already experienced. To dream into being any other reality than that which actively holds them down each day.

At the same time, we wish to acknowledge prison residents' ability to use this pain and this struggle as the force that will inspire within them to discover their own greatest strengths.

"Tears shed for another person are not a sign of weakness. They are a sign of a pure heart."

~JOSÉ N. HARRIS

That within these suppressive circumstances, they alone shape how they interact with life. This is the work of the imprisoned, to experience prison from the standpoint of the penitent, or the monk. Though their environment may be unjust and inhumane, we do not label them as victims of their circumstances. At the same time that we work to transition prisons into monasteries, we work to support those who are imprisoned to find the beauty inextricably present in all conditions.

The incarcerated individual's reality is one you see outside you every day. Now, let's turn inside, to what you experience within your own heart.

"The darker the night, the brighter the stars, the deeper the grief, the closer is God!"

~FYODOR DOSTOEVSKY

Acknowledging Trauma Among COs

"What you see in Corrections is this slow-rolling rock that continues to crawl over you and you don't even notice it," describes CO Greg. "It's an everyday, continual level of stress. It's a constant struggle to stay mentally sharp. It wears you down over time until you're just beaten. The support isn't there, and the people on the outside don't understand."

Similar to those in your care, COs experience a unique brand of stress. In addition to a low-level, ongoing threat of violence—those spikes when suppressed daimonic energy lunges forth, to which you must always remain vigilant—there are the terrifying moments when the dreaded actually occurs. As CO Andy described it, "You walk in on your first day and are immediately on this very intense, high state of constant alertness. When you grow up on the streets, like I did, that's a familiar feeling, but it comes and goes. You can leave that situation. But in prison, you can't, and it eats away at you mentally and physically. You can't decompress."

CO Brian said, "We have months on end of mundane routines doing the same thing every day. Then one day you come in and, five minutes after your shift begins, there's a shank at your throat..."

These are the obvious stresses—the threat of violence those of us on the outside conjure when we think of prison, or that we see in popular media. But there's also the stress of the grind. The sheer exhaustion. How your brain's ability to focus and stay alert wears thin due to ongoing stress and sleep deprivation. As CO Betsy Miller said, "There were a lot of COs working double shifts, four or five days in a row. Working excessive shifts led to significant emotional instability for COs. You could tell by how they treated the prison residents, often being overly aggressive. I found myself often getting irritable with my family from lack of sleep." In such circumstances, working long shifts with little to no chance for recovering, how can you be expected to cope long-term with the peaks and valleys of ongoing hypervigilance and moments of actual terrifying trauma?

As a result, your trauma travels with you. As a human being, someone who genuinely loves and cares for others, it's impossible to leave it all at work, as much as you try. CO Greg said, "When we go home at the end of the day, our loved ones ask how our day was. And just about every person inside these walls responds with, 'Fine.' We're trying to protect the people we love from what we've seen and heard. They're asking because they care and love us, but we don't want to talk about it. That friction builds up and eventually that connection is going to stop being there. Then, ten years into our career, nobody asks how we're doing anymore."

CO Chamelle agrees, adding, "This job is hard not just for the COs, but their families, too, and that often makes the COs feel even more stress because we know they are suffering."

What you see and experience every day, being locked up behind bars, surrounded by dense cinderblock walls, can leave you feeling less than human. As many COs describe, it can seem as if you're constantly carrying the weight of that world on your shoulders—this knowing and witnessing of the suffering that occurs in prison—and that who you are deep inside you has been somehow corrupted.

We won't belabor descriptions of your everyday experiences. After all, no one knows better than you. What we wish to do is acknowledge the trauma. To witness it. For too long, you've been told or intuited that what you hold inside you is too ugly

"I didn't know how to release the stuff I kept dreaming about. ... [Y]ou're watching a human being die in front of your eyes...and there's nothing you can do. Even though he's an inmate, he's still human; you're still human."

~CO MICHAEL, WHO HAS KNOWN NEARLY 20 OTHER COS WHO DIED BY SUICIDE, AND WHO NEARLY TOOK HIS OWN LIFES to be shared, and that you must carry it on your own, without comment and without complaint. But this is a strategy destined to fail, because again, life energy can only be suppressed for so long before it finds a way to express itself. You are not meant to become a casualty of suppression and suffering.

There's an ancient Japanese story about a devout monk who made a practice to leave the monastery regularly to meditate, and thus work to purify himself. One day, as the bustling sounds of the city below rose up to his ears, he found he was unable to focus on his meditation, so he decided to make the arduous climb to the shrine at the top of the mountain. It took him all day, but the absolute silence was worth it, and as the monk returned to the monastery, he vowed that he would return to the shrine every day until he was purified of all the ills of humanity. As he walked, he passed villagers in the mountains who beseeched him for help, but he kept walking because of a taboo on unclean people. Those in poverty or otherwise suffering, he and the other monks knew, could pollute you with the dark energy around them. The days passed and the monk traveled back and forth to the shrine, back and forth, all the while ignoring the suffering around him.

Then one day, months after he'd begun his travels to the mountain shrine, as the sun sank over the horizon and the air cooled, a sound came to the monk on the wind. The cries of a woman. "Help me. Please help me," he heard. Only this time, the monk was not able to ignore the sound of suffering. He tried to walk on, but somehow found himself turning in the direction of the cries. He came upon a woman outside a modest home, on her knees, crying. The monk knelt next to her. "Please," he said, "why do you cry so? What is it that you need? Food? Are you ill?"

"No," the woman said. "My mother just died, and I need help to bury her or her spirit will be forever imprisoned within her flesh."

The monk froze, for the taboo of touching the dead was the worst kind of pollution. If he helped the woman, he may never achieve true purification in this life or the next. But as he looked at the woman, he felt a warmth inside him that would not be denied.

"Alright," he nodded. "I will help you." And together, he and the woman ritually washed and prepared the old mother's body, then carefully buried it. The monk, himself, placed a cherry blossom atop the fresh mound of soil as an offering to the woman's spirit and a blessing for safe passage to the next realm.

The woman fell to her knees in gratitude, but the monk did not feel worthy of her praise. After all, he was now polluted. "Please," he said, casting his eyes away from her. In his shame, he turned and finished his walk down to the monastery.

When he arrived, strangely, all of the monks were assembled in the great hall. The monk learned that a great seer had arrived that afternoon and was preparing to bestow blessings on the most holy among them. The monk hid in the back of the hall behind a pillar as the seer scanned the faces of those present.

"You," she finally announced, pointing at the monk. "Please, come here." The monk knew he was found out. She had seen straight through to the darkness inside him and meant to make a spectacle of him. Slowly, he approached her. "Put out your hand," the seer instructed, and the monk did as he was told, expecting at any moment for her to take out a reed and begin to lash him for daring to reenter the monastery in such a state.

Instead, she reached out and took his hand in hers, then leaned forward and gently whispered into his ear a blessing so sacred that it cannot be repeated. Tears filled the monk's eyes as instead of shame, something else rose up inside him.

The next day, instead of making the pilgrimage to the shrine to work on his purification, the monk walked into the village, seeking out anyone he could find who was in need, and doing his best to help them. Beholding this, the other monks were aghast. How could he do this to himself? Yet because the monk had found true purity—the untouchable essence that resided unwavering inside him—he did not fear the sorrow and suffering of others, because he knew it could not change him. The monk did not try to explain this to his brethren, for he knew it was only by walking their own path and discovering their own purity that the other monks would understand.

We acknowledge that some part of you has suffered deeply, and we understand that this is precisely because you care. Because your heart, your essence, are not in alignment with a system that dehumanizes. That you hurt when others hurt. That you cannot resist the call to compassion and care, regardless of how others might judge you or how society may turn its back on you. We acknowledge the incredible nobility of your actions and intention and the love and service and loyalty that fuel them.

The Possibility

Myths and fables are powerful tools because they not only impart lessons and insights, like the tale of the monk they also help us glimpse possibility. While what will actually come to be in our own life is a story yet to be known, myths show us something akin to what our own lives can look like. They inspire and stoke the fires of imagination.

Even though the vision we hold for our lives will probably not look exactly like what we imagine, by allowing ourselves to create or connect with a vision in the first place, to dream is an affirmation of the possible. It shows that we believe in ourselves, and that we're starting to put some trust in ourselves and in life that if we show up, if we contribute our energy and attention, our deepest gifts will in fact be revealed.

You've probably already glimpsed possibility in your day-to-day work. The individual who tips you off to potential trouble. The prison resident or fellow CO who thanks you for listening to them. Even simply having a conversation with a prison resident about the upcoming playoffs. Simple moments of humanity shared are among the most subtle but powerful portents of possibility.

Then there are the glimpses of possibility becoming reality. At some prisons, new approaches are being taken that engage residents in true rehabilitative activities. In Maine, for instance, incarcerated individuals learn to grow vegetables and cook healthy meals for themselves from scratch. In New York, some new prisons are being designed to provide a physical atmosphere that enlivens instead of punishes. In pockets of North Dakota and Oregon, prisons are being restyled to incorporate education and skill-building programs and provide warmer, more comfortable living facilities for residents. You are not doing this imagining, this envisioning, alone. There are others out there who are lending their energy, knowledge, and gifts to change the system.

This transformation may seem far away. It often feels lonely when you're alone on the vanguard, trying to bring into being a world that others don't yet see. This is part of the work of the Guardian, as well—being the vision-bearer for a world in which those who are incarcerated are embraced and supported, and those who care for them appreciated and honored.

"Be a lamp, or a lifeboat, or a ladder. Help someone's soul heal. Walk out of your house like a shepherd."

~RUMI

CO Andy said, "I've had a lot of good experiences. On my last day at the prison, roughly ten guys met me at the door and were basically like, 'Hey, good luck to you.' There aren't a lot of handshakes and hugs that go on in prison. That was as close as I could get to feeling like I had done a fair job at coaching where I can, mentoring, and trying to be an example." And yet Andy's path to this point was not easy, and was often obscured by the struggle around him, which he internalized. "I treated others badly in the first part of my life," Andy said. "When it came to abusing myself with alcohol and everything else, it took the hand of God to get me out of it. When you're given a pass like that, you are not letting that go. I believe I am now in a place one could only dream of, with a family that loves and supports me unconditionally, that knows everything there is to know about me and still accepts me. I meditate. I pray. I have a strong faith. I can walk through a doorway and have complete faith that it's the right doorway spiritually, physically, and mentally."

Early in Andy's life and his career, he felt offtrack. Misguided. And yet he was never actually off his path. It was simply that all of the twists and turns made it impossible to see what was ahead. Similarly, you, too, are on your path. In this very moment, you are exactly where you are supposed to be. Take a second and glimpse the possibility all around you, right now, in this moment. It may come to you as a memory, a thought, a body sensation. It doesn't matter what form it takes, just let it come and simply observe it. Right now, there is no need to do any more than that.

How Disappointment Compounds Trauma

There is a disappointment you expose yourself to in working with those incarcerated, particularly when you are offering yourself to try to help someone along their own transformation. People can take two steps forward, and one step back. Sometimes three steps back. Sometimes it's two steps forward and all you see afterward are backward steps. These are heartbreaking, particularly when you've invested yourself.

One of the paradoxes of life is that possibility seems like a future event, but in actuality, it lives in the present, in this very moment. In your work as a Guardian, you don't need to concern yourself with what happens tomorrow, the next month, or the next year with a prison resident, or with yourself. Visions of the future can help to fuel and motivate us, but we want to hold them lightly, because the future will never be exactly as we hope or plan. And if we limit the future to the confines of our vision, no matter how grand, in a way we're also restricting what can be.

Also, when we create rigid goals, we risk disappointment. And when we feel disappointed, we are fixated on one potential outcome and missing all others. When we fixate, we begin to create a blockage.

Growing up, as very young children we learn to look to those around us, usually our primary caregivers first, and then other adults, to confirm our worthiness and the correctness of our behavior. We judge our properness and our goodness by their responses. Do they smile or frown? Are we rewarded or punished? These experiences create the narrow guardrails within which we act going forward. We're judged for whether our test garners an A or a D, and we thereby internalize the idea that the result of our work is the measure of our worth. That our presence and our effort are only meaningful if they engender a certain outcome.

"The ultimate lesson all of us have to learn is unconditional love, which includes not only others but ourselves as well."

~ELISABETH KÜBLER-ROSS

You've probably had an experience by now where you've invested time and attention in someone—be they a loved one, a colleague, an incarcerated individual, or someone else—hoping or even assuming that if you behave in the "right" way, they will speak or act in the way you want. And so, you've probably also experienced the frustration of this approach as things didn't go the way you'd planned. We are not formulas. People have their experiences, motivations, and paths and so you may have done everything "right" according to some set of calculations, but others still can respond in a way that disappoints you. This makes you feel unworthy, or ineffective. Possibility fades as you fixate on how your narrow-desired outcome did not come to pass. Once again, you find yourself facing confinement, this time in the walls of your own mind as you judge yourself. From this space, you're likely to judge others harshly, as well.

Rabindranath Tagore wrote, "The one who plants trees, knowing that he will never sit in their shade, has at least started to understand the meaning of life." One of the tasks of the Guardian is to unlearn the transactional, conditional way of relating to others that most of us learned growing up. It is not the role of the Prisoner to give back to you, or to validate or provide feedback on your performance. It's true that you will see changes all around you, at work and at home, and elsewhere as you embody your true self. Yet as much as possible, try to unlink what you see and experience from any form of assessment or validation on "how you're doing."

The goal is to see unconditionally—to look beyond illusions to see who others are in their deep, true essence. It's a difficult task for most of us because again, most of us have never experienced truly unconditional love or generosity. The challenge is not to learn how to see unconditionally, because this is a knowledge you already have that is being suppressed. The challenge is to notice where the barriers to expressing this natural state exist, and to gently remove them, or better yet, simply allow them to dissolve. To *let* yourself see the best in people.

> *"Unconditional love really exists in each of us. It is part of our deep inner being."*
>
> ~RAM DASS

The purpose of your work is not the product. It is not what happens as a result of your work. The purpose of your work is to do the work. To do the work is to be who you are. To embody your genius. Then let go of the outcome. By embracing the Guardian inside you and bringing your full self to life, you fulfill your purpose.

Releasing both the past trauma you have experienced and the future that may be, the only question you need to ask at any given time is this: *What is possible now, in this moment?*

Integration Exercises

Take some time to read again the acknowledgment of trauma for incarcerated individuals, then allow yourself a few quiet moments to sit in stillness. There is no agenda for this time other than to be. If discomfort or grief arises, that is okay. You can allow it to be and to move through you without judgment. Think of the grief as an affirmation of your love and your aliveness.

Take some time to read again the acknowledgment of trauma for COs, then allow yourself a few quiet moments to sit in stillness. There is no agenda for this time other than to be. If discomfort or grief arises, that is okay. You can allow it to be and to move through you without judgment. Again, think of the grief as an affirmation of your love and your aliveness.

- Where in your life have you feared or felt the sensation of being polluted or otherwise tainted or broken?

- What moments of possibility have you experienced as a CO?

- What do you *sense* is possible as a Guardian? Try not to limit yourself to what you think is logically possible, but listen to all of your senses, including your body, to feel into what is possible, no matter how nonsensical or unlikely it may seem. Remember to hold every possibility lightly, like a small bird, so that you do not unintentionally limit what may come to be.

STORIES FROM
CORRECTIONAL OFFICERS

The following pages have stories from Correctional Officers who, like you, have gone through this program. They tell their story of who they are, what drew them to becoming a Correctional Officer, and the impact of the job on their lives. As you know, most Officers do not share their stories. They do not have a place where they can talk about or write about their experiences. We share these here so you know there are others like you, who have gone through similar journeys and found themselves here, on the path *From Guards to Guardians*.

Gary

Gary York

I was in the Army for ten years, where I served in the Military Police, and when I got out I became a Correction Officer in the Florida State prison system and Investigations for 28.8 years. Being a CO is hard, many people can't handle that job. My brother has been a street cop for twenty-three years and has faced many dangers, but he said that he wouldn't work in a prison. I think it takes a special person to get locked behind the walls, outnumbered a hundred to one, with no weapon. It can be dull and boring one second and then, all of a sudden, out of nowhere, there's a riot, a fight, some kind of disturbance.

When I got out of the Army I was twenty-eight years old and I had some useful life experience. But even so, when I got into my Correction Officer uniform and was told, "Okay, here's some keys and you're stationed at dorm one, two, and three," it was a shock. When the doors close behind you and you're in the prison, it's a different feeling. You've got to deal with a lot of anxiety, fear, injuries, and even PTSD after a while. When I started, we didn't even have mace on our belt. There were about forty-five inmates in each dorm, and there I was, alone, in charge of all these inmates, and without any weapon. So I can only imagine what it must be like for a nineteen-year-old fresh out of school.

When you're new, the inmates are going to watch every move you make. You can't show any fear, because, if they see you're afraid, they're going to try to manipulate you. They take advantage of weak Officers and laugh at them behind their backs. You do one favor for one person and all of a sudden the inmate has leverage over you. You have to be careful, because your kindness is easily taken advantage of. It affects your humanity in a way and causes you to harden. I think I was pretty fortunate, because I made it clear from the beginning that I was going to make the inmates follow the rules, but I would also be fair. Once they see you're fair, they leave you alone. In addition, I was really good with interpersonal communications and treated the prisoners as people no matter the crime. I presented tasks in a way that allowed them to feel human. I wasn't just another RoboCop barking orders. A lot of people think that if you say thank you to an inmate you have belittled yourself. Well, if the inmate just cleaned up the whole dorm, I was going to say thank you for doing a good job. They appreciated that acknowledgment of their humanity.

When you're working in a prison system, you see inmates killing other inmates, you see inmates committing suicide, you see inmates attacking Officers, killing Officers, hurting some Officers badly. During my time as a Corrections Investigator, I had to go to several autopsies, and after the first couple of corpses, I got numb to it. One time, I even walked in with my cup of coffee, and when I was reminded that wasn't allowed, it kind of woke me up to how normal sitting in on autopsies had become for me—how much of my own humanity was shut down after years on the job.

During investigations, when inmates were killed, I was usually the one talking to their parents. You're there talking to them and letting them know what happened to their child. Seeing the parents' reactions, you can't help but feel for them. As a father of five, I couldn't help being impacted by those conversations, and there were times I took those emotions home with me. I would talk to my wife, who helped work through them. Not everyone has that kind of support, and a lot of COs like to keep things to themselves.

At the other extreme, I've seen an inmate bite a piece of an Officer's face off and tell him, "I have AIDS and now you do too." That inmate was transferred to another prison, and the Officers there were informed of what he'd done. That inmate was then beaten for five days and eventually passed away from his injuries. I've investigated many cases like that, and I never condoned that kind of behavior on the part of COs, because it can really turn into an Us vs Them situation, which only escalates tension. Being a Correction Officer is a dangerous job and you don't always know how to prepare for every situation you will encounter. Toward the end of my career, I was getting burned out from the job. You never know the mental, in addition to the physical toll it takes on you until you've been through it.

I say this because it is important for Officers to learn how not to bring the job home with them. It's one of the most stressful jobs there is, and to reduce the stress, when you walk out the door at the end of your shift, you need to let the job go and live your life. It can be hard sometimes, but if you can do it you'll survive a long career in Corrections. My wife also did 35 years in Corrections, and we made a deal with each other that we would do that. Sometimes we needed to vent and we would go on long walks to talk things through, clear our heads, and protect the kids from what we were experiencing. We did whatever we could to live a normal life outside work, whether that meant cooking dinner or going out to the movies—things of that nature. I am lucky to have a wife in Corrections with whom I could share my problems and know she understood. We had one another's back.

After a long career, there are a couple of things in the system I would like to see change. I think new young Officers need to get more training in ethics and inmate manipulation, because I believe that many of them who get into trouble aren't actually crooked or bad; they just didn't know any better and fell into the trap that was set for them by inmates. But, In addition to proper training for young Officers, I think there are other issues the prison system needs to address. Many of these are simply providing humane living conditions for the inmates.

Really bad riots have been triggered by basic problems like overcrowding, sanitary conditions, and just the quality of the food. The prison population may be criminals but they are also human beings. They want a clean place to live, something reasonable to eat, and they don't want four people living in a cell made for two. So if inmates are complaining about these kinds of things, the administration needs to pay attention, because they are warning signs. A lot of them are frivolous, but some are serious, and if you don't deal with them, the inmates may deal with them in their own way. Some people are going to say, "Well, why should we cater to these inmates?" But the thing is, you're not catering to them; you're trying to prevent a riot that's going to put everyone in danger.

And finally, not just new Officers, but everyone working in the system needs to have emotional and psychological support. I also believe they should have some type of exercise program and physical therapy to keep them healthy and in good shape. Many agencies have someone in human resources you can go to if you need help either emotionally or financially, but many don't. Correctional Officers need someone to talk to in a crisis situation. It's not that different from being in the military and seeing your buddy get killed in the field. Post-traumatic stress disorder is real, and it needs to be addressed. We need someone to talk to after witnessing something like that.

Gary, father of five children and grandfather of five more, received the Army Commendation Medal and Soldier of the Quarter Award during the 10 years he served in the Army. The first job he held during his 28.8 years in the Correctional System was at Hillsborough Correctional. Next he went on to the Polk Correctional Institution, and from there he spent 12 years as an investigator for the Tallahassee Central Office. In that job he was sent all over Florida doing investigations. And finally, he went to work at the Polk County Sheriff's Office for another 12 years. Gary also received the 'Correctional Probation Officer Leadership Award' for Region V, Tampa, Florida, 'Correctional Probation and the Outstanding Merit Award' for leadership in Region V, Tampa, Florida. Since then he's retired and written two books, Corruption Behind Bars *and* Inside the Inner Circle, *based on his experiences. Now he's working on a third book called* The Toughest Job.

Michelle

Michelle Threatt

I started in Corrections and law enforcement in October of 2002 at Hardee Correctional Institution where I worked until 2006. I then moved on to the Polk County Sheriff's Office until my retirement in 2017. I came into the field because there was a prison being built near me and they were looking for Officers. My mom didn't want me to go into law enforcement. She said once you get behind those gates, you're locked up, too. Those words would ring true later. She passed away in June of 2000 and I started thinking about it more seriously.

I had been working with juveniles at a detention facility and one of the supervisors was watching how I built my relationship and rapport with the delinquent juveniles that were always in trouble, and how I could reach out and talk with them. He told me I would be a good fit in the prison system and suggested I go down to Hardee Correctional and apply, which I did the following week. They called me a few days later to tell me I had the position.

Hardee Correctional was a closed prison. We had a lot of lifers, all males. The first day I walked into those gates and they shut behind me, I looked around at all of the inmates in their uniforms and the fear just hit me. I was thinking, oh my God, what have I done? The first inmate to ever speak to me walked up and said, "Officer, what's your name?" I told him and he said, "Tomorrow when you come in here, you show no fear. Because it's all over you."

I thought about that my entire shift while I was in training. When I got home, I kept thinking about the fear that I showed walking onto that compound, seeing all these men and knowing that some are killers, rapists, sexual predators... I opened my Bible and read the scripture, "I am wise as a serpent, but calm as a dove." I memorized that scripture and told myself then and there that I was wise and would remain calm. The next day I made up my mind that I could do this. I held my head up. I kept saying that scripture in my mind and the fear left me. I never had that issue again.

It never really got comfortable there because you always had to be mindful and aware of where you were. You were with men that have killed. Some of them take it as a form of disrespect to ask what they are in there for, but others are willing to tell you. I never wanted to know because if you knew, you might not want to talk to them. That's where judgment comes in and I wanted to be fair regardless of the crimes they committed and have been punished for. Some would never see freedom again. Some inmates would talk to me and I would get this eerie feeling. I would always look them up to see what they did and in every single instance the inmate was a rapist. You pray you go home safe to your family but you never know what situations might occur.

I had one inmate transferred from the prison because his actions had become possessive. They aren't around any women, so they'll get used to you and in their mindset, because you talked to them, you now belong to them when all you are doing is your job. I didn't feel safe with things this inmate would say. As women, we would deal with them gunning us. Gunning is when they bring out their private parts and they're masturbating out in the open. It didn't matter if other men were around. Sometimes they'd do it while we were counting and they're standing at the door with their private parts out masturbating at you. The very first time that it happened to me, I was on the court and there were five of them standing there. This one guy was just doing his business and I told him he was going to jail, which inside means confinement for 30 days. They put the cuffs on him and locked him up. I would ask, "Do you realize what you are doing? You are mentally raping me." We're supposed to be calm and respectful, but I thought it was absolutely disgusting and I let them know it. Some will come back and apologize to you. Some will apologize and do it again.

I didn't have any physical altercations at Hardee, but later at the sheriff's office I did. I now call it the "best worst day of my life." When it happened in 2010, I thought it was the saddest, craziest thing ever. I was on a hospital watch with an inmate shackled to the bed and he wanted to get up. I handcuffed his hands, shackled his feet together with the shackles, and let go of the handcuffs from the bed. I can't recall if I backed up, or if I turned, or what I did, but the next thing I remember was seeing blood on the wall.

He had been in the hospital maybe three or four days and had gotten the gooseneck faucet out of the bathroom. He was hitting me on the side of my head with it. I recall looking at his feet wondering if I was getting sick because all I saw was blood everywhere. He said that his plan was to bash my brains and get my gun to kill me and whoever got in his way.

I'm a true believer in God. I knew God had me as we fought. He was on the third floor and we made it to the hallway and he was naked and sweating. The nurses tried to get me to stay and these two guys who were visiting jumped on top of him. He was acting like he was possessed. He got loose from them and was running down the hallway. I took off behind him and the nurse told me to stay back because help was coming. But the only thing I was thinking was, *That's my job running. That's my career right there.*

When I got to the stairs, I made a choice not to shoot and just took him on. By the time I got outside I could hear the helicopter and the sirens. The sergeants pulled up in their car and asked which way the inmate went. I pointed them in the right direction and then I passed out right there on the street. When I awakened, a nurse was assuring me I wasn't going to die. I had staples in my head and a concussion. To this day my hair never really grew back in that area. I thought that was the worst thing that could have happened because I couldn't understand why someone would want to kill me for no reason.

After that incident, I went through a lot mentally and emotionally that I tried to hide because I didn't want people to know what I was going through. That I saw his face every day for years. After my attack, doctors diagnosed me with PTSD. I was put on Xanax. I didn't sleep for four days. I kept thinking he was going to attack me. I came home one day and my bathroom door was locked. I thought someone was in there. I ran out and called 911 screaming and they knew it was me. They were thinking maybe it was the inmate's family trying to get back at me. They sent out the cavalry. They had shotguns and dogs and the street was blocked. There were Officers everywhere. They got in the bathroom and saw it was just the lock on the door. I had an anxiety attack. I was embarrassed. That's when I realized something was really wrong with me. I had tried to hide it from my family because I didn't want them to think I was crazy. I didn't want to tell them I'd be driving down the road and see his face, or that I'd look over in my passenger seat and see him.

I was angry with my job. I was angry with my supervisors. I was just angry. I was angry with that inmate for wanting to take me from my family. I was just getting ready to get married. Some would hate him, but I didn't because it ended up all for a reason. I worked through it with the workmen's comp site doctor, my own personal doctor, and a sheriff's office mental health doctor. I would talk about it with my doctors and in my culture our grandmothers would tell us to talk to the Lord, but that the Lord also gives us people to help. Prayer is wonderful, but there are people here on Earth to help us through it. Those doctors helped me and prayer just works.

I heard God say to stop taking Xanax. I didn't take it anymore. My body was craving it. I wasn't even having an anxiety attack and wanted to take it to feel calm. I realized this is how people get addicted because I was having the feeling like I needed to take the pill, but I stood strong. I refused to be addicted and just needed to learn when the anxiety attacks would come on and practice my breathing.

I wouldn't have wished that incident on anyone. At that time I wore a hair weave and still ended up with staples. If that had been one of my coworkers that didn't wear a weave, he would have hit them straight on their head, gotten their gun, and killed them while they were passed out. Years later I wondered why it was me. People always ask why they have cancer or why this or that. My question now is, why not me? I'm glad that it was me because that seed he [the inmate] planted pushed me into my purpose. I still call it the "best worst day of my life" because everything changed for the better. People ask me how I was able to forgive him so easily. It's because of the good that came out of it.

I ended up receiving a Purple Heart from the sheriff's office, the Medal of Valor. Earlier that year I had saved an inmate from choking and was up for Detention Deputy of the Year. I've always done my best and taken pride in every job. After I left detention, I went into the communications department with that same commitment. I'd be on the phone with people who found their loved ones deceased from suicide and stay on the call with them. I've cried with my coworkers when we got a bad call, it's hard to not take that call home with you and think about it. One of my coworkers on another shift did commit suicide. I was only aware of three Officers that did commit suicide in my 15 years in law enforcement. I myself never thought about it.

At the communications department, I received one call about a young man who killed himself. His friend found him, then his mom showed up on the scene. You have to stay on the phone until a deputy gets there. There is a professional protocol you must follow. I'm on the phone, listening to the screaming, the crying, to the mother that just found her child. I would listen with tears rolling down my face. Then when I hung up, I would go outside and cry or scream because it's hard not to be compassionate. It's hard not to be human. But it takes a toll on you mentally and with how you relate to your family.

At that time, I was married and because you are so professional and in-charge on the job, you would take that same tone with your family. I would find myself speaking to my now ex-husband and my sons and they would have to remind me they were not my inmates. I had to work on it because you don't even realize you are doing it until it's brought to your attention. But my marriage was over by then. We already had some issues and that didn't help. We got divorced in 2016 and after leaving law enforcement, I really got control over it because friends told me about my actions and my tone. It broke me down because it hurt me to know that at times I did it with them, too.

When I left the communications department to retire in 2017, I didn't have a full plan. I had always enjoyed cooking, but had no money to start anything big. I started cooking on weekends and got my first food truck in 2019. Then COVID hit and I was sitting in my prayer room and heard God say as clear as day, "I need you to feed these kids." I had $13. I said, "I don't know how I'm gonna feed them for $13." He said, "Just do it." I thought of a meal of fried hot dogs, chips, some drinks, and some sweets. The next day, a friend of mine called and said he had something for me. It was hot dogs. I thought, oh my God, you've got to be kidding me! Someone else called me that owed me money. I was able to buy everything for that first Wednesday and we fed 74 kids.

We had to shut down during the lockdowns, but I made an announcement on my social media page that I was going to do it again. By the following Tuesday, because we do it every Wednesday, people had donated $600. Each week people were donating from all over. Someone called the newspaper and they did a story. We ended up being able to do it from March until August. We fed almost 3,000 kids. We had teachers and different volunteers every Wednesday. Some prayed with the kids. Some helped them with their homework.

Now people are volunteering their time, including different organizations. I named the feeding of the kids "The Village" because so many people came together to help. It has just been the most humbling experience that I've ever had. I tell people all the time my food truck is my career and inspiring others and helping my community is my purpose. So many people, when they go through something traumatic, choose to wallow in that. I did not choose to. PTSD is real and it's something awful but you have to be strong and know who you are. I refused to let that incident kill me. I always tell people, I'm not going to let that inmate hold me back because if he had not attacked me, I would still be in that uniform. I wouldn't be feeding kids. I wouldn't have a food truck.

I've grown so much over the last four years. I know that everything—the bad, the good, and the ugly—all works together for good no matter how bad it might seem. I found purpose in sharing my story and inspiring others. I found purpose feeding these kids. I have my book about my life moments to inspire, laugh, and pray. Without the "best worst day of my life," I would never have thought it possible I could become an author. I am going to eventually write about my experience with the inmate. I'm just waiting for God to move me on it. I don't know how long I'll be doing this food truck because I think I have bigger plans in store. God always provides every time. We just have to listen. Two weeks ago, I woke up at 5:00 AM and I heard him say, "There are three things that move me: faith, obedience, and sacrifice. So, you're going to have to remember that—faith, obedience, and sacrifice, no matter what it looks like." I'm just so excited about all the doors that God is opening for me.

Michelle Threatt has been dedicated to law enforcement in Polk County, Florida for over 15 years. She has received numerous accolades for saving an inmate's life, and in 2010 Michelle was honored with Detention Deputy of the Year, the Purple Heart, and the Medal of Valor. Following retirement, Michelle started feeding the kids in her community. "The Village" has given out more than 4,000 meals since, feeding over 2,450 students. The community honored her with the Action Partnership Community Service Award for outstanding support and commitment from the Agricultural and Labor Program and the Polk County Community. Michelle authored Life Moments to Inspire, Laugh, and Pray, *where she shares about her life.*

Brian

Brian Dawe

I started as a state Correctional Officer at MCI Norfolk medium-security prison in Massachusetts in May of 1982 and left the department in 1998. In 1988, I helped co-found the Massachusetts Correctional Officers Federated Union, and served on the executive board for nine years. During my tenure, I started connecting with the Officers around the country, sharing universal concerns and addressing issues we all have in this business. Utilizing those connections, I set up a network called the American Correctional Officer Intelligence Network, which I've run since the mid-nineties. Recently, I merged my organization with One Voice United, founded by Andy Potter, a retired Correctional Officer out of Michigan. Our two organizations have very similar concerns, and it seemed like a perfect fit to put the two together. In August I assumed the position of National Director for One Voice United.

We often come to this job for the economic necessity, for the benefits. By my second year, I loved what I was doing and thought I was doing something good for society. When I first started, Officers had a say. If there was a classification hearing, when the inmate was going to be considered for lower security, they would bring us in and ask for our opinion. The same used to be true for disciplinary or parole hearings, our opinions mattered. We don't do any of that anymore. We are just warehousing. We hold them until their sentence is done and try to make sure that no one gets killed. When one inmate tries to kill or injure another inmate, we get in the middle and stop it and usually neither one of them dies. Whether it's an assault, a medical emergency, a fire or a riot we are the first, last, and only responders behind those walls.

I became jaded by the system when I realized we're not about correcting; we're about making sure they don't get out until they're supposed to. That diminishes our roles as Correctional Officers. I started medicating heavily with alcohol to cope. After my fifth or sixth year, it started to get worse. I drank heavily for about five years. Being a CO is probably one of the toughest mental jobs there is. When I started, I ran a housing unit for 44 convicted felons and myself. When I left, it was up to 66. You're in a constant state of hypervigilance where you must always be on, even with all the downtime. The biggest problem is that things can go from zero to 160 in seconds.

We have months on end of mundane routines doing the same thing every day. Then one day you come in and, five minutes after your shift begins, there's a shank at your throat or one of your brother's or sister's throat, and you better be able to react properly and immediately. That type of stress takes a tremendous toll physically and mentally. We have a high suicide rate, twice the number per capita of what police officers have. We have 156 estimated suicides per year. It's a very demanding job and we get no accolades. People don't realize the toll that can take on us, especially since we don't talk about it a lot.

Family and friends will tell me I'm not the same person I was when I started the job. I count the change now when I leave the store. If I go into a restaurant, once I sit down and I look around, I realize I have positioned myself so nothing can come behind me. It becomes instinct and that shouldn't be natural. You don't trust people like you used to, you start to believe everybody's trying to con you, inmates and management. All we have left is each other. We won't talk to our families about what we see and what we have to do on some days. It's just not something you share at the dinner table. It builds up inside you and there's very few release valves, thus the high divorce rates, alcoholism, substance abuse, opioid use, painkillers, in our ranks. It's devastating. We have a 34% PTSD rate. That's beyond epidemic and no one's paying any attention to it. Maybe the only way anyone's going to care is when they start to realize the economic cost, which is tremendous.

We now have 60% of the inmates coming into the prison system with mental health issues. We're not trained in mental health. They shut down our mental health facilities in the eighties and at the same time they started the war on drugs. The increased population made the job so much more difficult and made rehabilitation virtually impossible. It affects our mental health, too. There are no movies or TV shows that show how we put our lives on the line for guys that may have been put away forever, but we get in there and we do that every day. Where are those stories? You never see that stuff. When you don't have that type of recognition or any job satisfaction, it wears on you, it makes you feel worthless.

There is a lot of personal stress, not just PTSD we deal with. It's not a disorder for us. It's PTSI, it's an injury. It's a post-traumatic stress injury caused by the job. When you say disorder that implies that you have some personal control over that, like an eating disorder or alcoholic, that's not the same here. This is a brain injury from the trauma we deal with day after day and what we see and hear, because we all work in the same basic environment. When you have an Officer that is murdered or taken hostage in Colorado or Minnesota or wherever, that has a huge ripple effect throughout the entire Corrections community. Every single one of us knows that next shift, it could be us, and our families know it, too. The trauma we suffer is not just individual, it's collective.

Fortunately, I've never had suicidal thoughts, but I know people who have. I had a very good friend, a sergeant. He was a trainer for one of the organizations I worked for. We were all at a conference and we started talking about wellness and he raised his hand. He told us about the day his son, who was also a Correctional Officer, walked in on him when he was sitting on his kitchen floor with a gun in his mouth. He was this happy-go-lucky guy. You never had any inkling he was dealing with demons. It floored us.

It opened the floodgates, though, and people started talking and that's what we need more than anything. Our job says you can be small, you can be heavy, you can be tall, you can be short, you can be of any religion, race, or gender, but you can't be weak. When it comes to dealing with the stresses of the job it's a catch-22. You need the help, but if you go to get help, you can lose your job. So, what do you do? 156 of us commit suicide every year. We drink ourselves to death. Many can become physically abusive. We all know when we sign on that this job comes with physical danger, but they don't tell you about the danger to your mind and spirit. Over time you begin to lose your natural tendencies toward human empathy and compassion, a part of your humanity is slowly whittled away.

When you have 11 Correctional Officers die in the line of duty across the country each year, but you have 156 take their own lives, you have to ask, "Where's the real problem?" Is it the inmates? Or is it the job? It's the job. But that's good news, because that you can control, that you can change. That is what we're trying to do now, and the first thing we must do is educate our managers and get them to change. In the culture of Corrections, if you have a prison that's run poorly, don't look at the Officers, look at management. The way we're trained and the way a prison runs is a direct reflection of the people who run it, not the people who carry out the orders. Corrections is a paramilitary organization. Policies and decisions are made top-down.

Surviving behind the walls comes down to respect. If you are firm, fair, and consistent and maintain a respectful relationship with the inmates most of the time that respect will be returned. You can also find out a lot of stuff that can save your butt. I remember one time at MCI Norfolk I had just arrived at my housing unit and was about to head upstairs to do a check. One of the inmates in the housing unit turned to me and mouthed the words 'be careful.' Earlier that day when I was heading into work, I noticed there were more Officers than normal in the parking lot. I thought it might be a training exercise, but when I went upstairs to roll-call, we were told it was getting a little rowdy inside. We were warned that we may have a couple of situations and to be especially observant and cautious.

We hit the quad and there had to be maybe 300 inmates walking around. I went to my housing unit and relieved the Officer on duty. I asked if he was going home, he said no, they were going to reassign them. I read my logbook, counted my keys, and made sure I did my check. Everything was good. I was about to make my round when the inmate mouthed those words to be careful. Just as I'm heading up the stairs the Lieutenant comes in and says, "Get your log, get your keys, lock the office door, and get outta here. Go and head to the ad building." I did exactly what he said, and I remembered "be careful."

As I'm heading to the ad building, I hear through the gates all the guys in their tactical gear coming in and behind them come the dogs. Behind them come the guys with loaded firearms. We took that place back in an hour. We had that place back under control. Not one person got hurt, not one Officer, not one inmate. It took us two days to get the people who were really causing all the problems moved out of there. I didn't go home for two days.

But no one got hurt and that is not something you hear about on the news. There is so much negative stigma of what goes on behind these walls. Bureau Justice statistics did a study on prison rape, and it comes out close to what you see on the streets. I am not downplaying it, it's horrendous when it does happen. But most things people are told that go on in Corrections are overblown and people judge us on that false narrative.

On a separate occasion I put myself in a situation that I had to think long and hard about for a long time afterward. I was responding to a fight between two inmates and it could have cost me my life. About thirty inmates had surrounded the two combatants and I didn't let my training take hold. I jumped in and pushed my way through when I should have waited for backup. I'll never know if I emerged unscathed out of the respect I had in the unit or if it was just luck, but I was very fortunate that I didn't have a real problem.

I've seen inmates come to an Officer's rescue more than once. The good stories are the inmates that don't come back, when one of them makes it good. It's also good to see the things that my brother and his sisters are doing that people don't know about, like all the charity work. These people go out and work in their communities. When I was with the union in Massachusetts, we used to do an event every year for abused mothers and children. There's a lot of good stuff that Correctional Officers do around the country that no one ever hears about.

I was lucky that in my personal life, my wife and I reconciled after being apart. I also stopped drinking. As of today, I haven't had a drink in 13/14 years. I tried to stop before for my family, but if you're an alcoholic, you're an addict and unless you are ready to stop for you, you won't stop. I'm grateful that I've had my sobriety and it's a much better way to live, but I'm still a statistic when it comes to Corrections in that the abuse got to me.

I hope that people will take a little more time and consider who we are and what we do. I wish we could mandate that politicians go to prison, go to a state facility or a county jail on a Friday or Saturday night. Make them spend four hours with line staff in uniform like a rookie and go to the chow hall, walk the yard, do a headcount. Then draft your legislation and make reforms because we want reforms too.

We don't want these guys to come back, but we can't do our job if we don't have the staff or if we're not trained to properly help with the rehabilitation process. So, let's use the staff we have and train them properly and get staffing ratios to where they should be so that we can give these guys and gals a chance, so they don't have to come back. Let's take this opportunity of reform to deescalate. Let's take this chance to train our Officers better, not just in hand-to-hand combat, which we need to know, but let's train everyone in emotional intelligence, learning how to deescalate situations quicker, better, faster, more consistently.

That's what One Voice United is—a voice for reform for those who work there and as a result who live there. There are many areas where we want the same results as many other stakeholders do although our motivations may differ. Everybody in the reform movement thinks private prisons are a bad idea. Great, we do too, let's get rid of them. Everybody in the reform movement agrees that inmates need more programs. Everybody agrees that we should separate the mentally ill inmates and put them in a situation where they are not in so much danger and they have a chance for success and to get treatment. We all want more effective training, better de-escalation skills and wellness programs that affect everyone in Corrections. Those are reforms that Officers, the incarcerated population, families, and inmates' rights groups agree with.

We need pre-hiring psychological screening, and the pay and benefits must be commensurate with what the job is. From day one, when they hit the academy, cadets need to have a mentor, someone they can speak to about the problems behind the walls, about dealing with the internal bullying, and about the pressure of the catch-22 of not being weak and having someone to talk to. We must set something up for their families so that they have help, and follow our Officers throughout their careers and train them every year in new de-escalation, emotional intelligence, and stress coping skills. Then they can communicate better with the inmates and among themselves and make it a safer place for everybody.

We need a plan for those who will soon retire and ask them if they are interested in staying in the field, maybe mentoring children, maybe going to boys' and girls' clubs, or mentoring new Officers that come on board. We must give retirees the psychological help they need. Our suicide rate after retirement is depressing. The estimated suicide ideation rate of retired Correctional Officers is 17%.

Mortality rates of Correctional Officers are between 59-61 years old. We give up nearly 20 years of our lives to do this job. The very least society can do is give us the tools to live a little bit longer and improve our well-being.

Brian Dawe started his career in law enforcement as a State Correctional Officer in Massachusetts in 1982. He is a cofounder of the Massachusetts Correction Officers Federated Union where he served on the executive board for nine years. He is also the founder of the American Correctional Officer Intelligence Network, which he recently brought under the One Voice United umbrella. He earned his Bachelor of Arts Degree in Criminal Justice from the University of Massachusetts and currently lives in the Boston area. In August 2020 he accepted his current position as the National Director for One Voice United. He is a father of two and grandfather of two.

Andy

Andy Potter

I began my career as a Correctional Officer in the late 1980s working at the Michigan Training Unit. I also worked at a maximum-security facility called Oaks Correctional Facility and then I transferred back to the training unit. Currently, I serve as the executive director for the Michigan Corrections Organization. I'm also the founder of One Voice United, working with a lot of Corrections groups around the United States to help them navigate their way to the front of the conversation around Corrections issues, reform, and things that will affect their work for the next five or 10 years.

I grew up in the 1980s in a very small town with very few options for a future. Many of us were in and out of trouble growing up, myself included. Higher education wasn't an option for us. This was when there was a huge emphasis on getting tough on crime, the whole "say no to drugs" thing. They were starting to incarcerate more and more people, so the prison industry was growing.

For me, Corrections seemed to be a good profession, with a pension, good health care, and relatively good pay. It was a pathway into the middle-class. When you can get into an industry or a profession where you can possibly make a difference in somebody's life, that becomes a part of your choice, and it certainly was for me. I talk to a lot of new recruits and most say it would be great if they could make a difference. Sadly, the light in their eyes goes out between the time they go into the academy and when they go through those front gates to work on the first day. That light is gone because the system makes sure that it's not part of the deal. Corrections were never initially designed or built for success in the rehabilitation of inmates.

When you come in, you are trained and conditioned to be desensitized. You have very little space to be vulnerable. People come in and say that it's not going to change them, and they are going to be different. But it does change you. You walk in on your first day and are immediately on this very intense, high state of constant alertness. When you grow up in the streets, like I did, that's a familiar feeling, but it comes and goes. You can leave that situation, but in a prison, you can't, and it eats away at you mentally and physically. You can't decompress. I tell new recruits that if you let it, this will get a hold of you and wreck you in a hurry. It can make you very thick-skinned and opinionated. You can't walk into a mall or a restaurant or a crowded theater without feeling that heightened alertness. You sit with your back against the wall and that is not normal.

The first half of my career was the hardest. I've asked myself if I have PTSD and yes, I do. Even now, and I've been out of the system for years, it comes back in certain circumstances to a point where I can recognize and understand it. In the beginning, I didn't understand or even recognize it. Frankly, I didn't want to admit it. It's not something that Corrections Officers readily talk about. They don't sit around and discuss it. They do sit around and try to one-up themselves with stories and different things. Maybe that is their way of coping.

When you work in that environment all the time, you become very cynical and non-trusting. I always think somebody has an ulterior motive. I have daughters that I constantly worry about, knowing what is out there. Even how I am with them is affected. For example, I was going into my daughter's school once and she pulled me aside and said, "Dad, can you take that line out of the middle of your eyes for a minute?" I was surprised because I was in a good mood and having fun but to others my appearance looked angry. My daughters have told me countless times that their friends don't like coming around and it's caused problems because I'm not as trusting as I could be. I tend to call people out if I think they're lying, and I can be pretty raw about it. My wife always says, "Can you say it in a way that allows them an out, gives them a place to go? You can't just corner them and say hey, I don't think you're telling me the truth." For my family to have to ask me to be more approachable to people proved this was something I needed to work on.

It causes problems with how you allow people to approach you and communicate with you without feeling like there's an ulterior motive. The one thing that's stolen most from Corrections Officers is their ability to be vulnerable. As the saying goes, you can't really experience love unless you allow yourself to be completely vulnerable to it and to what comes with it—the hurt, the joy, and everything that can be a part of a much more amazing experience. It's a travesty really.

Dealing with inmates is another issue where you can have a bad experience based on how you approach it and how you carry yourself. A lot of Corrections Officers say that if you show them respect, you'll get respect in return. That's not human nature and it's not realistic. The reality is that your interaction is met differently moment to moment because there's so many different individuals that are incarcerated, and you must recognize as soon as you can where their attitudes are at.

I've had bad experiences. Before I retired, I had this growing sense in me that I probably wouldn't make it out alive. I have been through a lot. I had been hit in the head with padlocks and suffered other injuries. However, this time I started getting this feeling and it wouldn't go away. That was a heavy weight on me until I decided it was time for me to go and I'm glad I did.

I've never had suicidal thoughts, but I lost some people I grew up with to suicide in the department. I've been in a situation where I've had their family come up to me, maybe the mother of someone I grew up with, crying and asking what can be done about it. What do you say to somebody that lost a child you grew up with? I had one friend who was in the department for 20 years and in good physical health, other than chronic pain from being injured over and over. When someone like him goes to the doctors, the intention is to bring him back to work as quickly as possible. They give out pain meds and maybe a short period of physical therapy and they bring him back.

He did rehabilitation and got off the pain meds. He came back to work like a new man. Six months later, he got injured again and was back on pain meds. A week later he died of an accidental overdose. He had little kids, and it wasn't that he wasn't trying to do his job the best he could. He took an oath and he tried to live up to that. There is a set of expectations that come with this job that are tough on people.

Sometimes there are signs, but you react to them a little too late. Corrections Officers don't pry into each other's business or dig into things. But when they do, they come together. We can scrap and argue with each other, there's a culture of that, but when the shit hits the fan we're shoulder to shoulder, we lock arms, whether inside of a prison or outside. When you "roll around in blood with someone," it's hard to not see that person differently. When there are situations that can take your life at any second and you roll around in blood with somebody and they had your back, then every time you cross the sidewalk with them, every time you go through a doorway with them, every time you see them, there's a sense that only you can understand each other. It's the same for people that go through combat. They recognize each other for life. That's not normal or healthy.

I've had a lot of good experiences. On my last day there, roughly 10 guys met me at the door and were basically like, "Hey, good luck to you." There aren't a lot of handshakes and hugs that go on in prison. That was as close as I could get to feeling like I had done a fair job at coaching where I can, mentoring and trying to be an example. Working with inmates, COs don't get to see a finished product. If I could go home at night and tell a story about how I helped somebody, or I made a difference in some way, then I think COs would feel more fulfilled.

I went through many things that brought me to a place in time where I reflected on all the hurt I had done to people the first half of my life. It wasn't the hurt that I did to myself. It was the hurt that I did to everybody around me that was revealed to me in a way that could only be from God. I thank God every day because he snatched me right out of hell and allowed me to scrape my eyes clear so I could truly see what things were and who I was. It allowed me a chance to be vulnerable enough to self-reflect and find the pathway back from all that hurt and damage. When I met my wife in the latter part of my career, I had already moved away from self-medicating into a much healthier lifestyle. I believed in a higher power, which made a world of difference, and I understood the impact of that. I knew there was something else out there.

Through my own years in Corrections, I've managed to take this all apart layer by layer and evaluate it. I've seen the pendulum swing over the course of 30 years from warehousing people to attempting to rehabilitate. None of it really includes the voices of COs or frontline staff. If we're going to reform Corrections, or any other system, you need all the stakeholders. Corrections Officers are the second largest stakeholder and they're left out of this conversation. They are just going to be handed a policy one day that says their work has changed and now here is what they have to do. There's no buy-in for them.

We must acknowledge that PTSD is really an injury, not a disorder. It is an injury, something that's brought on to you. It's not something that's already inside of you. I pushed back on the notion that it's a disorder based on research done in this field over the last ten years. Corrections Officers, unions, and others, myself included, drove that conversation. The system fights back when we try to get funding for it. We must push prison reform to a point where it becomes mainstream, with bipartisan support. It's a human investment that you pay for up-front, but the recuperation from that is undeniable.

I'm a great example of this return on investment because of how badly I treated others in the first part of my life. When it came to abusing myself with alcohol and everything else, it took the hand of God to get me out of it. When you're given a pass like that, you are not letting that go. I believe I am now in a place one could only dream of being, with a family that loves and supports me unconditionally, that knows everything there is to know about me and still accepts me, and it makes me understand those that don't have that, and have more empathy for them. I meditate. I pray. I have a strong faith. I can walk through a doorway and have complete faith that it's the right doorway spiritually, physically, and mentally.

My life's mission is to advocate for Corrections Officers and help them find purpose. People assume they know who we are and what we go through. Don't just take the Shawshank Redemption narrative because it's not reality. Corrections Officers want their profession to be recognized through a positive lens. They want to be proud of what they do. They want a system that supports them. These people are family members, part-time firemen, school workers. They aren't thugs. They are a part of your community. They are people you know.

Andy Potter is the Founder of One Voice United and the Executive Director of the Michigan Corrections Organization (MCO). He is a nationally recognized leader in the labor and economic justice movements, with particular expertise in worker rights and leadership development. Andy began his career as a Correctional Officer for the Michigan Department of Corrections (MDOC) where he worked for nearly three decades. He has held gubernatorial appointments on several task forces, including serving on the Michigan Corrections Officers Training Council from 2004 to 2013. He chairs several committees such as the SEIU National Conservative Member Engagement Committee, the SEIU National Corrections Council, and is a member of the Michigan State Council. In 2019 he was appointed to serve as a Vice President for SEIU's International Executive Board. Since 2015, Andy has been the Executive Director of MCO representing 6,500 Corrections and forensic security officers throughout the state of Michigan. During his time as Executive Director, Potter spearheaded several new initiatives that revolutionized Officer engagement and restructured internal operations to maximize the organization's impact and sustainability. The 21st century strategies that Potter implemented at MCO have garnered national recognition as a model for others to replicate. Currently, as the founder of the national non-profit organization, One Voice United, Andy is working to transform the criminal justice system by building bridges and unearthing common ground between all impacted stakeholders.

NEXT STEPS
(PROGRAM CONTINUATION)

By completing this book, you have taken your first step on the journey From Guards to Guardians. You may choose to read this book and answer the questions many times. If you find that you would like to take this work further, we have options available, based on what you would like your next step to be.

1. Work one-on-one with the program manager.

2. Go through this program in a group, where you can share your experience and hear the experiences of other Correctional Officers.

3. Work with a CO mentor, someone who has gone through this program who is available to guide you on your journey.

4. After you have completed all of these, you have the opportunity to become a CO mentor, guiding other Correctional Officers through their journey.

NOTES

Lesson 2

"12 Mythological Archetypes in Greek Myth," Know Your Archetypes, accessed July 30, 2023, https://knowyourarchetypes.com/mythological-archetypes/.

"Mary Johnson and Oshea Israel," The Forgiveness Project, accessed July 30, 2023, https://www.theforgivenessproject.com/stories-library/mary-johnson-oshea-israel/.

"A Walk," All Poetry, accessed July 30, 2023, https://allpoetry.com/A-Walk.

"The 12 Brand Archetypes," The Hartford, accessed July 30, 2023, https://www.thehartford.com/business-insurance/strategy/brand-archetypes/choosing-brand-archetype.

"What is Archetypal Psychology," Psy-Minds, accessed July 30, 2023, https://psy-minds.com/archetypal-psychology/.

Lesson 4

"Post-Traumatic Stress's Surprisingly Positive Flip Side," The New York Times Magazine, March 22, 2012, https://www.nytimes.com/2012/03/25/magazine/post-traumatic-stresss-surprisingly-positive-flip-side.html.

"'Prison Guards Can Never Be Weak': The Hidden PTSD Crisis in America's Jails," The Guardian, May 20, 2015, https://www.theguardian.com us-news/2015/may/20/corrections-officers-ptsd-american-prisons.

"Posttraumatic Growth: A New Perspective on Psychotraumatology," Boston University, April 1, 2004, https://www.bu.edu/wheelock/files/2018/05/Article-Tedeschi-and-Lawrence-Calhoun-Posttraumatic-Growth-2014.pdf.

"What is Post-Traumatic Growth," Positive Psychology, August 31, 2019, https://positivepsychology.com/post-traumatic-growth/.

FROM THE AUTHOR

I want to know life biblically, the way a man knows a woman, the way a lover knows a beloved. I want to know the water by getting wet. Theory, commandments, concepts leave me hollow. My driving questions when I come across dicta and dogma are, *Is that true? Is it wholly true? Where and how is it true? For whom is it true and why? Can it withstand the test of time? Is it true for me as a woman?* The last one has taken me off many a beaten path. Givens are often no longer givens when I ask this question. The world turns upside down. As a free woman, I want all things to be free, liberated from any ideas I would impose on them.

We are constructed of the divine. I believe everything—and I mean everything—when properly tended to, reveals an untold beauty. But my work is not as activist, reformer, saint, teacher, guru, or shaman—it is as artist. The art I do is akin to found-object art: art made from what has been thrown away. It's an art that turns something back into itself. Like turning prisons into monasteries; the degradation of addiction into the art of addiction that isolates the addiction drive for purposes of realization; the life sentence of trauma into human flourishing; the feminism of subjugated women into the feminine collective of inestimable power; those who have been canceled, exiled, and banished into the leaders of the next era; desertified soil into not only carbon-absorbing but nutrient-producing; hunger and food deserts into farm-to-table, free, pop-up restaurants; black culture into the black box for society that holds the secrets. These programs exist, and you can find them here: **www.unconditionalfreedom.org**.

My work remains as it always was: to turn poison into medicine and make it available to those who want it. But for those who need it, here is the conventional side of things: I graduated from San Francisco State University with a degree in semantics and gender communication. I cofounded the popular avant-garde art gallery, 111 Minna Gallery, in San Francisco's SoMa.

I have appeared on ABC News Nightline, and my work has been featured in *The New York Times*, *New York Post*, *San Francisco Chronicle*, and *7x7 Magazine*, among others. I've written for *Tricycle: The Buddhist Review*.

www.ingramcontent.com/pod-product-compliance
Lightning Source LLC
Chambersburg PA
CBHW052113020426
42335CB00021B/2743